SYLVIA

SCREENPLAY AND INTRODUCTION BY
John Brownlow

A Newmarket Shooting Script® Series Book

NEWMARKET PRESS • NEW YORK

FIRST EDITION

10 9 8 7 6 5 4 3 2 1

ISBN: 1-55704-615-8 (paperback)

10 9 8 7 6 5 4 3 2 1

ISBN: 1-55704-616-6 (hardcover)

Library of Congress Catalog-in-Publication Data is available upon request.

QUANTITY PURCHASES

Companies, professional groups, clubs, and other organizations may qualify for special terms when ordering quantities of this title. For information, write to Special Sales, Newmarket Press, 18 East 48th Street, New York, NY 10017; call (212) 832-3575 or 1-800-669-3903; FAX (212) 832-3629; or e-mail mailbox@newmarketpress.com.

Website: www.newmarketpress.com

Manufactured in the United States of America.

OTHER BOOKS IN THE NEWMARKET SHOOTING SCRIPT® SERIES INCLUDE:

About a Boy: The Shooting Script
Adaptation: The Shooting Script
The Age of Innocence: The Shooting Script
American Beauty: The Shooting Script
Ararat: The Shooting Script
A Beautiful Mind: The Shooting Script
The Birdcage: The Shooting Script
Blackhawk Down: The Shooting Script
Cast Away: The Shooting Script
Dead Man Walking: The Shooting Script
Dreamcatcher: The Shooting Script
Erin Brockovich: The Shooting Script
Gods and Monsters: The Shooting Script
Gosford Park: The Shooting Script
Human Nature: The Shooting Script
The Ice Storm: The Shooting Script

Igby Goes Down: The Shooting Script
Knight's Tale: The Shooting Script
Man on the Moon: The Shooting Script
The Matrix: The Shooting Script
Nurse Betty: The Shooting Script
Pieces of April: The Shooting Script
The People vs. Larry Flynt: The Shooting Script
Punch-Drunk Love: The Shooting Script
Red Dragon: The Shooting Script
The Shawshank Redemption: The Shooting Script
Snatch: The Shooting Script
Snow Falling on Cedars: The Shooting Script
State and Main: The Shooting Script
Traffic: The Shooting Script
The Truman Show: The Shooting Script
U-Turn: The Shooting Script

OTHER NEWMARKET PICTORIAL MOVIEBOOKS AND NEWMARKET INSIDER FILM BOOKS INCLUDE:

The Age of Innocence: A Portrait of the Film★
Ali: The Movie and The Man★
Amistad: A Celebration of the Film by Steven Spielberg
The Art of The Matrix★
The Art of X2★
Bram Stoker's Dracula: The Film and the Legend
Catch Me If You Can: The Illustrated Screenplay★
Chicago: The Movie and Lyrics★
Crouching Tiger, Hidden Dragon: A Portrait of the Ang Lee Film★
Dances with Wolves: The Illustrated Story of the Epic Film★
E.T. The Extra Terrestrial From Concept to Classic—The Illustrated Story of the Film and the Filmmakers★

Frida: Bringing Frida Kahlo's Life and Art to Film★
Gladiator: The Making of the Ridley Scott Epic Film
Gods and Generals: The Illustrated Story of the Epic Civil War Film★
The Hulk: The Illustrated Screenplay★
The Jaws Log
Men in Black: The Script and the Story Behind the Film★
Planet of the Apes: Re-imagined by Tim Burton★
Saving Private Ryan: The Men, The Mission, The Movie
The Sense and Sensibility Screenplay & Diaries★
Stuart Little: The Art, the Artists and the Story Behind the Amazing Movie★

★*Includes Screenplay*

CONTENTS

Sylvia Plath

Gwyneth Paltrow as Sylvia Plath

INTRODUCTION

BY JOHN BROWNLOW

When in mid-2000 Alison Owen, producer of the acclaimed *Elizabeth*, first mentioned to me that she was interested in making a film about the life of Sylvia Plath, I immediately felt my screenwriting antennae begin to twitch. She told me that it was a project she had been thinking about for years, but that the literary establishment was largely against it and that many writers were reluctant to get involved.

Then there was the problem of the poetry. The literary estates of Sylvia Plath and Ted Hughes were thought to be unlikely to co-operate with a movie, and that meant there was a risk they would not sanction the use of any of the poetry in the script. Finally, the Plathites and the Hughesites were involved in a feud of the order of Godzilla vs. Mothra. Hughes was regarded by some as a murderer. Others took the view that Plath was a hysterical self-dramatist, possibly psychopathic, and vastly overrated as a poet. Whatever line it took, the film would almost certainly become the meat in a sexual/political/poetical sandwich.

For all these reasons, it appealed to me enormously. I told Alison and the head of BBC Films, David Thompson, that I would love to do it, but that I wanted to be sure there was a story there. What I meant was that I wanted to be sure that there was a film here that was not dependent on the audience being interested in Sylvia Plath.

What was this story going to be about when it was not about poetry? I re-read all the biographies and felt depressed and confused. They all told a different story, and they all seemed to take a polemical stance, pro-Plath or pro-Hughes. Hughes's own *Birthday Letters* told a fairly clear story, but it was cerebral, undoubtedly self-serving, and possibly unreliable. In any case, we would not be able to get the rights to it. Plath's poetry and journals told another story, but it wasn't reliable either, and again the rights problem was a brick wall.

I couldn't see a story. But I now felt sure there was one. So we hired a researcher with whom I had worked extensively on documentaries, and she went off and did all the biographical research again. When I looked at the new material, the story was blindingly clear. This wasn't a story about two poets, or more precisely, it was only incidentally a story about two poets. It was a love story between two giants. Hughes and Plath had done something that most of us only dream of: they had met their soulmate, and married them. But it was a marriage that only one of them could survive.

Outlines and treatments are the screenwriter's secret weapons. Many screenwriters, to my amazement, resist them. I often insist on having a treatment or step-outline stage written into my contract. The reason is simple. Screen narrative is not about writing dialogue and writing action descriptions. It is about events, and the order in which they take place. The outline stage presents you with an opportunity to prototype the story until you get it right. It ensures that everyone in the film-making chain knows what to expect. And it forces you, as the writer, to nail your vision of the film in a simple, declarative form.

On the basis of the new research, I outlined heavily, then wrote a full studio-style treatment, thirty or forty pages, using only real events from their marriage to dramatise the story that I sensed lay beneath their poetry and their lives. The outline was approved and I commenced the first draft.

I find it helpful to have another film in mind when I start writing, even though the finished project may not resemble it in any way. In this case, my model was *Who's Afraid of Virginia Woolf?,* where a couple who love one another rip themselves to pieces as others become unwitting victims in their co-dependent psychodrama. I imagined the parts in my movie being played by Richard Burton and Elizabeth Taylor. I even called it, in my own head, *Who's Afraid of Sylvia Plath?*

I knew it had to be a romantic film. And because the ending was going to be gruelling and tragic, I knew the front had to be light. You had to have a reason to believe that these people were capable of happiness. And there had to be humour. In *Hamlet*, you are always grateful for the grave-diggers, and in my script Sylvia's tormented last days are alleviated by her relationship with the professor who lives in the apartment below hers, wonderfully played in the film by Michael Gambon. I also felt that Sylvia's self-absorption needed to be tempered by a sort of gallows humour, ever present in Plath's own journals, which prevents the audience from losing sympathy with her during her bleak last days.

My biggest anxiety was dialogue. I simply could not work out how I was supposed to ventriloquise conversations between two of the twentieth-century's greatest literary talents. Then one day I read that Hughes said he had only ever heard Plath utter a metaphor once in casual conversation. I suddenly realised that when Sylvia Plath and Ted Hughes were doing the washing up, they didn't speak in verse. From that point on, wherever possible, I cut dialogue and if I couldn't cut it I made it as banal as I could, while ensuring the situations were dramatic. It's an old trick, used to perfection by both Harold Pinter and David Mamet in their screenplays. As the dialogue is peeled back, the subtext carries the story, and the film begins to live.

Then there was Sylvia. Depending on who you read, Sylvia Plath was variously perfectly normal, oppressed, manic, depressive, manic-depressive, schizophrenic, a borderline personality, a psychopath, a sociopath, a nymphomaniac, addicted to sleeping tablets, the victim of an Electra complex, a masochist, and very definitely a misogynist. Or was that a feminist? Then there was her paranoia, the effect of the electro-shock treatment, the malign (or was it benign?) influence of her mother. . . . The list was as long as it was unhelpful. The problem is that this kind of armchair diagnosis of characters never helps you as a screenwriter depict them as vital, living creatures. In fact, as soon as you settle on a diagnosis, all the life goes out of your characters.

So how do you depict mental instability? One of the things I learned from making documentary films is that people with mental troubles are fundamentally the same as you and me, except that very particular aspects of their personality are exaggerated. They may believe strongly something that most of us consider to be false—that they are God, or can fly, or that there are television cameras watching them the whole time. (On one spectacular occasion, I surprised someone who believed exactly this by turning up with a television crew. She locked herself in a cupboard until we went away.) Or they may become paralysed by sadness, or filled with extraordinary and baseless self-confidence.

Well, we have all been there. I have believed things that were entirely false. I have been paralysed by sadness. I am often filled with baseless self-confidence. The experiences of the mentally unstable may be more extreme than most of ours, but they are not categorically different. In terms of writing, you simply take whatever aspect happens to be exaggerated or different in the character you are writing, and then make sure their behaviour is entirely normal and consistent *given that difference.*

In *Sylvia*, we took pains to have Sylvia's actions make sense. We were very careful to leave the question of Ted Hughes's fidelity or infidelity open until he begins the final affair with Assia Wevill. You are never quite sure if Sylvia is paranoid to suspect him, or justified in thinking he's playing the field. Then, just as you decide that perhaps she is paranoid, he begins an affair. You are, in other words, in the same position as Sylvia, trying to figure out what's going on. We also tried very hard to let the audience in on Sylvia's particular psychodrama: her obsession with death and her father. There was nothing "mad" about this: for someone who has attempted suicide, death is a logical preoccupation. For someone who has lost their father, the desire to be reunited with him makes perfect sense.

The hardest part of the script to write was the ending. We knew we had to dramatise her decision to commit suicide, and to leave her children behind. But there was a massive danger that at that point that we would lose the audience. That you would simply not understand her reasons, or think she was selfish or stupid or "mad". On the other hand, it would be irresponsible to endorse her decision to commit suicide or to shrink from portraying the devastating effect it would have on her family. The only solution was to show that Sylvia's decision to take her own life was at least understandable, even if we did not ask the audience to endorse it.

We used an earlier, abortive, suicide attempt to show that Sylvia had taken a decision not to commit suicide, for the sake of the children. From that point on we showed her reaching out repeatedly, trying again and again to find ways out of the maze she found herself trapped in. The audience had to feel that every door had closed on her. We gave Sylvia and Ted a final reunion scene, mainly because I am absolutely certain that something like that happened, but also because we needed a moment of happiness and resolution before the final, fatal act. We also needed to feel the final door close on Sylvia.

The first draft took me four weeks, including a week to revise the first writer's draft. I delivered it and was astonished to learn that the producers were happy enough with it to go out to a director immediately. That was when I first encountered what I now realise is a general problem: The Curse of the Good First Draft.

No producer or director or financier, or indeed writer, can ever resist the desire to make a screenplay better. And all screenplays can be improved. Unfortunately, when a script is actually working fairly well at the get-go, it is much more likely that changes will take the script backwards, and that vast amounts of pain will have to be suffered and energy expended before it gets better again. In other words, you had better start taking your vitamins.

Director Pawel Pawlikowski (*Last Resort*) called me from his bath to tell me that he loved the script. Pawel, whom I already knew and liked and would unhesitatingly describe as a genius, was soon attached as director, and instantly brought a new sensibility to bear on the script.

Pawel's favourite phrase is "Hollywood bullshit" and he swiftly identified many areas of the script he felt were clichéd or rhetorical. In a series of some-times heated but very stimulating script meetings, during which I am alleged to have thrown a script across the room, we came up with a blue-print for a new draft that involved excising large amounts of narrative. Pawel wanted to concentrate on the high dramatic points and let the audi-ence fill in the gaps for themselves. I felt it was a high-risk move, but his vision was clear, and we all agreed it was worth trying.

When the script was delivered, the reaction was negative. It had improved in some areas, but it had become depressing and fragmented, and both Alison and I felt that it was no longer the movie we had set out to make. A third draft corrected some of these problems, but I still felt, without quite being able to articulate it, that in some indefinable way the script had lost ground.

Nevertheless the script went out to cast, and our spirits were enormously raised when Gwyneth Paltrow agreed to play Sylvia. Up to this point, it was still possible to think of ours as a small literary film. However, with Gwyneth on board, we were clearly in the realm of Hollywood. This was what I had always wanted for the film, but to Pawel it was troubling. He was no longer sure he was the right person to make the movie. Over beer in the pub one night, he muttered darkly about "Hollywood bullshit".

I was not surprised to get a call from Alison a couple of weeks later telling me Pawel had left the production in an amicable divorce. We now had a film with an A-list star, a green-lit script, a start date that was less than three months away. . . and no director. A frenetic six-week hunt followed. After pursuing several blind alleys, Christine Jeffs boarded the film like the Seventh Cavalry coming over the hill. I watched her first film, *Rain*, which I loved, and flew to England to meet her. We hammered out the basis of a new draft, which I returned to my home in Toronto to execute, while Christine got on with casting and pre-production.

All seemed to be going well until I delivered the script, at which point we had what every production has at some time or another: namely, a com-plete train wreck. Although the changes to the script were what we had all agreed, Christine and at least one of the film's financiers now felt that the script wasn't working. I re-read it myself, and knew in my heart they were right. It was competently executed, but the life had gone out of it.

Unfortunately, I had no idea how to fix it. What followed was a nightmare that I am still not ready to describe in detail, although it will make a fine chapter in a book one day when we are all dead or past caring. Three days of sleep deprivation, plotting, politicking and group psychosis that would have awed Machiavelli miraculously produced something like a consensus. We had to go back to the first draft.

There were many changes and cuts to be made, and many scenes to be meshed in that had improved in subsequent drafts, but the first draft had the tingle factor, a unity of intention and a continuity of execution, that we were missing. I would normally have scheduled four weeks for this work, but the situation was now so dire that if I did not deliver in three days a script that could be approved by producer, director, financiers and star, we would not hit the necessary milestones to make our start date, which was in turn fixed by cast availability. In other words, the production would probably fall apart.

I went to my hotel room and took the phone off the hook. I typed continuously for three days and three nights. I took one hour to sleep each night and half an hour to go for a walk. I drank copiously and charged it to the financiers. I figured they owed me at least that. When I delivered, everyone pronounced themselves happy and the film moved on into production. I flew home and collapsed.

Sylvia was one of those defining moments that only happen a few times in your life. That moment of walking into a set that appeared to have been plucked wholesale from my cerebellum will stay with me for ever. I'm now, at the time of writing, looking forward to my first premiere. I may even buy a second suit, rather than wearing the one I wore at my wedding. The last time I went to L.A. for meetings, I found myself being ushered through those studio gates that five years previously I had stared at from the outside. I still get a little thrill from driving on to the Paramount or Warner's or Universal lot. I think once you lose that thrill, it's probably time to quit the movies and become a pig farmer. Which I still might, one day.

Sylvia also taught me a very important lesson, which is this: I want to direct. While I like screenwriting, and will continue to write for other people, there are some scripts that you feel so deeply that handing them over to other people is too painful. *Sylvia* was like that. People warned me at the beginning that I would feel this way, and I shrugged. Well, they were right.

SYLVIA

written by

John Brownlow

Sixth Draft, Fifth Revision

December 2002

OA   INT. AURELIA'S HOUSE - BASEMENT - DAY   OA

BLACKNESS. SILENCE. Then, just discernible, SHALLOW
BREATHING, a disturbed HEARTBEAT. Just the slightest
traces of light, like daylight filtering into a dark
cellar.

Now a WOMAN'S VOICE, a real East Coast twang, like
Katherine Hepburn, only more sarcastic.

                    SYLVIA (V.O.)
          [Sylvia quotes from her poem
          "Lady Lazarus," lines 43-48]

Then vague NOISES, as if something is being moved aside,
a pile of wood maybe. MUFFLED VOICES. Light, SPEARING
into the blackness. A confusion of SHAPES. Something
FLASHING. A SIREN. And now the BLACKNESS flickers into:

OB   INT. AMERICAN HOSPITAL ROOM - DAY - 1953   OB

BRIGHT WHITE LIGHT. The concerned faces of a middle-aged
woman (AURELIA PLATH), a NURSE, and a jowly DOCTOR, who's
holding an orange rubber tube attached to a STOMACH PUMP.

They are all of them peering into camera.

                    SYLVIA (O.S.)
      Oh, no.

1   EXT. CAMBRIDGE - DAY   1

SUPER: CAMBRIDGE, ENGLAND, 1956

Early morning. England of the 1950s: shades of gray and
shit-brown, cars that look like hearses, PEDESTRIANS in
austerity clothes hunched under the weight of a thousand
years of history.

Only now, hurtling towards them is an American girl
(SYLVIA PLATH) with a big flashing grin, her tyres
skittering and shuddering underneath her as she barrels
down the hill almost out of control.

It's clear from her face she's in love with the feeling.

She looks totally foreign, a splash of colour in a
monochrome land. Even the bicycle looks different, and so
it is, brand new and brightly colored like the girl's
lips and coat and shoes.

She radiates charisma, this girl, along with intensity
and a fierce intelligence.

                              (CONTINUED)

1   CONTINUED: 1

But strangeness too, and an off-kilter frequency that
puts the English on their back foot. An oddly charming,
oddly bewildering combination of convention and
unconvention, that says: "I am special. I am going to BE
someone".

Sylvia pumps along past a crowd of PEDESTRIANS, the usual
mix of town and gown, TWEEDY STUDENTS and OLD-AGE
PENSIONERS.

But now amidst them, she glimpses an EARNEST LOOKING
YOUNG MAN (Tom Hadley-Clarke) who is unsuccessfully
hawking MAGAZINES out of a leather satchel to the
shoppers.

Sylvia wobbles as she sees him.

                    SYLVIA
          Tom! Tom!

Tom looks up at the voice. Seeing Sylvia, he stuffs his
magazines into his bag, and hurries off in the opposite
direction, clearly wanting to avoid her.

Sylvia skips off her bike and starts to push it through
the pedestrians --

                    SYLVIA (CONT'D)
          Excuse me! Excuse me, please!

-- only to find Tom gone.

Now she spots him, a little way off, moving through the
crowd. She dumps her bike against a college wall with the
hundreds of others and sets off after him again.

5   EXT. CAMBRIDGE - COLLEGE GATES - DAY   5

Sylvia finally catches up with Tom.

                    SYLVIA
          Where is it? The magazine.

                    TOM
               (keeping the satchel
                away)
          Got held up at the printers.

                    SYLVIA
          I saw you selling them!

                    TOM
          Oh, that's right... sold out.

                                                     (CONTINUED)

CONTINUED:

His bulging satchel tells another story.

> SYLVIA
> They didn't review me, did they?

> TOM
> Oh, no. They reviewed you all
> right.

He pulls out a magazine, hands it to her.

> TOM (CONT'D)
> Poetry, page eleven. It's not
> very flattering.

Sylvia finds the page. Her face darkens with fury.

> SYLVIA
> (reads)
> "Superficial... bougeouise...
> commercial... nakedly ambitious"
> (to Tom, furious)
> Who the hell do they think they
> are?

> TOM
> You can ask them yourself.
> There's a launch party at the
> Women's Union tonight, eight
> o'clock.

5A   EXT. CAMBRIDGE - COLLEGE QUAD - DAY   5A

Sylvia pushes her bike into the quad, the magazine in her
basket. Her face. The words have stung her.

5B   EXT. CAMBRIDGE - COLLEGE QUAD - DAY   5B

Sylvia's bike, parked. Sylvia reads the magazine, leaning
on a parapet. She still can't believe the review. But now
she turns a page, idly skimming, and her eyes light on
something else.

Sylvia reads.

An epiphany.

When she looks up, the world is entirely different.

7   INT. CAMBRIDGE - WOMEN'S UNION - NIGHT   7

A riotous student party.

The place is dark, and crammed with WANNABEE BEATNIKS with experimental facial hair, mingling with PUBLIC SCHOOLBOYS in tweeds. There aren't too many GIRLS, and the ones there are doughnutted with blokes.

In one corner, a FOUR PIECE BAND is blowing deafening, raucous JAZZ. In front of them, partygoers are dancing the night away with a typical student combination of bacchanalian abandon and crease-browed concentration.

She enters, as if dressed for a high school prom. She looks at once strikingly beautiful and utterly out of place. We suddenly realize how tall she is compared to the other girls.

She scans the room like a searchlight, spots something on the others side of the room and sets off as if on a mission.

In another part of the room Tom, the boy who sold Sylvia the magazine, is jiving with a DOE-EYED GIRL in black. He's pretty drunk.

            TOM
        (YELLING as he jives)
    So you see the documentary films
    of Grierson represent a genuinely
    subversive expression of militant
    social consciousness...

Suddenly, here's Sylvia. She too has to yell.

           SYLVIA
         (to Tom)
    Is he here?

           TOM
    Who?

Sylvia realizes she is sticking out like a sore thumb not dancing, so joins in. Her style of dancing is unconventional to say the least, though not without a certain alien grace.

           SYLVIA
       (brandishing the
       magazine)
    The one who wrote this.

(CONTINUED)

                              TOM
                    What, that stuff about you?

                              SYLVIA
                         (jabbing at a poem)
                    No, this. This poem. Edward
                    Hughes.

                              TOM
                    Oh, Ted? He's over there.

Sylvia follows his gesture, and stops dancing.

It's the man in black.

He's a couple of years older, and even taller, with big
shoulders and floppy hair that droops over one eye, and a
mouth perpetually ready to curl into a smile. He scans
the room with a predatory, lupine air.

Sylvia, bang in front of him.

                              SYLVIA
                    I read your poems.

                              TED
                         (yelling over the
                          music)
                    WHAT?

                              SYLVIA (CONT'D)
                         (louder)
                    I SAID... DANCE WITH ME.

Ted grins a lupine grin.

They begin to DANCE, the RAUCOUS JAZZ deafening, whirling
around. As they dance, Sylvia YELLS poetry at him, Ted
equal parts amused, flattered, astonished, and aroused by
this extraordinary woman.

As the music CRASHES to an end, Ted pulls her off the
dancefloor, to another part of the room where the crowd
is a bit sparser.

                              TED
                    You learned my poems?

                              SYLVIA
                         (shakes her head)
                    I didn't have to. They stuck.

Ted locates a bottle of brandy and dumps it into two
glasses, hands one to Sylvia.

                                              (CONTINUED)

>   SYLVIA
>   As soon as I saw them I knew they
>   were the real thing! Big crashing
>   poems! Not blubbering baby stuff
>   like the others.

>   TED
>   You like?

>   SYLVIA
>   I like.

>   TED
>   Who the hell are you?

>   SYLVIA
>   Plath. Sylvia Plath.

Ted chokes on his brandy.

>   TED
>   The one whose poems...

>   SYLVIA
>   ...YOU tore to shreds.

>   TED
>   Not me. It was the editor.
>   (off her scepticism)
>   He must have known you were
>   beautiful.

>   SYLVIA
>   You mean I have to sleep with him
>   to get a decent review?

>   TED
>   Don't waste yourself on him.

Their eyes lock. You can practically taste the sex
between them.

>   TED
>   You're all there, aren't you?

>   SYLVIA
>   Yes, I am.

Ted glances round. An obviously English girl (his
GIRLFRIEND) is at the door, scanning around for him.

>   TED (CONT'D)
>   I have obligations in the other
>   room.

                                        (CONTINUED)

Seeing the tang of jealousy on Sylvia's face, on impulse
Ted leans forward and kisses Sylvia, hard, on the mouth.

The kiss has astonishing power for both of them, so much
so that when they part, Ted opens his palm to discover he
has pulled off her earrings and headband.

> TED (CONT'D)
> I shall keep these.

Sylvia's eyes, surprised at his audacity.

Over his shoulder she sees the girlfriend heading through
the throng towards them. She puts a hand behind Ted's
head and pulls him towards her. She kisses him again and
then, almost lovingly BITES hard into Ted's cheek.

Ted pulls away in shock. He reaches to his cheek,
discovers there is BLOOD there. He is about to say
something, but the furious girlfriend has reached them
now and YANKS him away.

12   INT. SYLVIA'S ROOM - DAY   12

CLATTERING OF A TYPEWRITER as WORDS pour onto a page.
Sylvia at her desk. She hesitates, bites her lip. Then
attacks the keys again.

> SYLVIA (V.O.)
> [Sylvia quotes from her poem
> "Pursuit," lines 1-2]

12aA   INT. SYLVIA'S ROOM - DAY - LATER   12aA

-- belonging to a HOUSEMATE of Sylvia's (DOREEN) who's
lounging in a chair, smoking, and reading Sylvia's latest
opus with a critical eye.

> DOREEN
> Bit morbid isn't it?

> SYLVIA
> He's my black marauder.

> DOREEN
> Well, I wouldn't get your hopes
> up.

> SYLVIA
> (pouncing on her)
> Why? What have you heard?

(CONTINUED)

12aA   CONTINUED: 12aA

> DOREEN
> Him and his crowd, all they care
> about is poetry. Anything else is
> a distraction. Including steady
> girlfriends.
> > (off Sylvia's look:
> > "but I'm different")
> Even pretty American ones with
> Fulbright scholarships and red
> bicycles.
> > (handing back the poem)
> What else? Oh yeah. He lives in
> London, and he'll screw anything
> in a skirt.

12A   INT. SYLVIA'S ROOM - DAY - LATER   12A

Sylvia lies on her bed bouncing a TENNIS BALL off the
wall and catching it.

> SYLVIA
> (with each throw)
> Edward Hughes. Ed. Ed Hughes.
> Ted. Ted Hughes. Ted Huge. Ted
> and Sylvia. Sylvia Hughes.

She bounces the ball off the wall with finality and sits
up.

> SYLVIA
> Sylvia Plath.

16   EXT. CAMBRIDGE - BACK GARDEN OF HOUSE - NIGHT   16

Tom and Ted, drunk from a long night in the pub, stumble
NOISILY over a fence and through a hedge into a back
garden. An unkempt lawn, rose beds. A light burns in the
window of an upper room of the house.

> TED
> Which one's hers?

> TOM
> (picks a random window)
> That one.

> TED
> How do you know?

Tom gives him a pitying look.

Ted bends down and picks up a clod of earth, lets fly.

                                              (CONTINUED)

16   CONTINUED: 16

SPLAT. It misses.

He does it again. SPLAT! it misses.

And again. SPLAT!

Ted, raining clods against the wall, missing every time.

Now a LIGHT flicks on and a window opens. DOREEN appears
at the window, yells:

                    DOREEN
          What the bloody hell do you think
          you're doing?

17   INT. CAMBRIDGE - HOUSE - NIGHT   17

Sylvia, returning from a walk, climbs the stairs up to
the attic landing. A DOOR OPENS to reveal Doreen.

                    DOREEN
          He was here.

                    SYLVIA
          Who?

                    DOREEN
          Your black marauder. Him and his
          little playmate, legless,
          chucking clods at my window.
          Thought it was yours, apparently.
          I told them if they didn't bugger
          off I'd call the police.

                    SYLVIA
          You talked to them? What did they
          say?

                    DOREEN
          Nothing comprehensible.

Sylvia's face falls. She moves towards her door. Doreen,
feeling bad for her. She produces a muddy, crumpled piece
of paper.

                    DOREEN
          But he left an address.

She grabs the scrap of paper and envelops the astonished
messenger in a huge transatlantic hug.

                    DOREEN
          Steady on there.

18   I/E. OVERGROUND TUBE TRAIN - DAY   18

Sylvia, travelling into London. Full of anticipation, she
watches the light flash between grimy Victorian brick
buildings. her face reflects in the window, overlaid with
changing images, now light, now dark, going faster,
faster...

19   EXT. RUGBY STREET - DAY   19

A three story building on a Bloomsbury street. Somewhere
someone is practising JAZZ TROMBONE. Sylvia checks an
address on a scrawled piece of paper, finds the house.
She gathers up her courage, knocks on the door. The
Trombone music stops.

An extremely FAT MAN with a TROMBONE answers (MICHAEL
BODDY). He looks her up and down.

                    BODDY
          So you're her, are you?

                    SYLVIA
          Am I?

                    BODDY
          Apparently.
               (opens the door wider)
          He's downstairs.

Sylvia squeezes past Boddy and the trombone.

21   INT. RUGBY STREET - BASEMENT STAIRS - DAY   21

Sylvia, alone, descends a dank staircase. There are great
water stains on the walls, paper peeling off in chunks.
It is unbelievably squalid.

Now a door in front of her. She opens it into --

22   INT. RUGBY STREET - KITCHEN/LIVING AREA - DAY   22

-- a real old fashioned basement kitchen, the old serving
quarters. It is a shambles of blood and root vegetables.
But that isn't why she stops dead.

It's Ted. He's covered in blood. A dead ANIMAL, half
disembowelled, swings from his hands

                                              (CONTINUED)

CONTINUED:

                    TED
          It's a hare. I'm jugging it.
                    (off her stupefaction)
          You know, in its own blood.

                    SYLVIA
          This place... it's...

                    TED
          ...like the Maze at Knossos.
          That's what they say. Nobody ever
          gets out. They all get swallowed
          by the Minotaur.

                    SYLVIA
          I should have brought a thread.

                    TED
          It's too late for that.

23   INT. RUGBY STREET - KITCHEN/LIVING AREA - NIGHT   23

On a table are the remnants of the jugged hare, with
empty plates and empty bottles all around.

Scratchy BEETHOVEN plays on a windup gramophone.

The diners, a bunch of Ted's bohemian friends (Tom from
the magazine, the corpulent BODDY, wild-eyed and wild-
haired MORECAMBE) are all lounging around in threadbare
armchairs, in states of inebriation beginning with
'legless'.

In the middle of the room is a table on which is placed a
HUGE ARRAY of improvised shot glasses -- wine glasses,
beakers, mugs, tea cups, egg cups, even old tin cans.

Tom stands, reciting poetry (NB: THE CHIEF DEFECT OF
HENRY KING by HILAIRE BELLOC) at ludicrous speed, trying
not to make a mistake (an old Russian drinking game).

                    TOM
          ...at last he swallowed some which tied
          Itself in Ugly Knots inside.
          Physicians of the utmost fame
          Were called at once, but when they came...

Meanwhile, Ted is in a private conversation with Sylvia,
in a passion about something.

                                                    (CONTINUED)

23   CONTINUED: 23

> TED
> It's magic. I don't mean <u>about</u>
> magic, or <u>like</u> magic, it IS
> magic. Real magic! Not conjuring
> tricks and rabbits in hats!
> Incantations, rituals,
> ceremonies, spells – what are
> they? Poems! So what's a poet? A
> shaman, that's what he is!

> SYLVIA
> Or she.

At that moment Tom stumbles on a line.

> EVERYONE
> Drink! Drink! Drink!

Tom takes a tin can, drains it, sits. Boddy stands and
begins reciting (GUNGA DIN by RUDYARD KIPLING) at
terrifying speed.

> BODDY
> (fast, music-hall
> squaddie)
> Now in Injia's sunny clime,
> Where I used to spend my time
> A-servin' of 'Er Majesty the Queen...

Ted, continuing where he left off.

> TED
> I tell you what, a good poem, a
> really good poem I mean, it's
> a...a... it's a bloody weapon.
> And not just a pea-shooter,
> either. A bloody atomic bomb.

> SYLVIA
> That's why they make you learn it
> at school.

Ted stares at her. What on earth is she going on about?

> SYLVIA
> They don't want kids messing
> about with it on their own. I
> mean, just imagine if a sonnet
> went off accidentally. BOOM!

Ted starts laughing, and now Boddy reaches the well-known
refrain, and all the regulars join in, including Ted,
banging their glasses with the metre.

(CONTINUED)

Sylvia, drinking it all in.

                         EVERYONE
              He was "Din! Din! Din!
              You limpin' lump o' brick-dust, Gunga Din!
              Hi! Slippery hitherao!
              Water, get it! Panee lao!
              You squidgy-nosed old idol, Gunga Din.

Boddy takes the next verse solo.

                         BODDY
              The uniform 'e wore
              Was nothin' much before,
              An' lather ress be'ind... <u>bollocks</u>!

                         EVERYONE
              DRINK! DRINK! DRINK! DRINK!

He does. All eyes turn to Sylvia, who has no choice but
to stand. Sylvia, suddenly realising this is a test.

                         SYLVIA (CONT'D)
                    (not fast)
              If it be you that stir these daughters' hearts
              Against their father...

                         EVERYONE
              FASTER! FASTER!

                         SYLVIA
                    (speeding up)
              Let not women's weapons, water-drops,
              Stain my man's cheeks! No, you unnatural hags,
              I will have such revenges on you both,
              That all the world shall -- I will do such
              things,
                    (very fast now, but
                     still perfectly
                     fluent)
              What they are, yet I know not: but they shall be
              The terrors of the earth. You think I'll weep
              No, I'll not weep: I have full cause of weeping;
              but this heart
              Shall break into a hundred thousand flaws,
              Or ere I'll weep. O fool, I shall go mad!

APPLAUSE. Ted stands. Sylvia doesn't sit down.

                         TED (CONT'D)
                    (insanely fast)
              O my love! My wife!
              Death, that hath suck'd the honey of thy breath,
              Hath had no power yet upon thy beauty:
                                                    (CONTINUED)

23   CONTINUED: (3)   23

>   Thou art not conquer'd; beauty's ensign yet
>   Is crimson in thy lips and in thy cheeks,
>   And death's pale flag is not advanced there.

APPLAUSE and CHEERS for the stunning speed of this.

>   TED
>   (normal speed)
>   Ah, dear Juliet,
>   Why art thou yet so fair? Shall I believe
>   That unsubstantial death is amorous,
>   And that the lean abhorred monster keeps
>   Thee here in dark to be his paramour?

It is as if there is no-one in the room with them now.

>   SYLVIA
>   For fear of that, I still will stay with thee;
>   And never from this palace of dim night
>   Depart again: here, here will I remain
>   With worms that are thy chamber-maids

>   TED
>   O you
>   The doors of breath, seal with a righteous kiss
>   A dateless bargain to engrossing death!
>   (a big swig of vodka)
>   Here's to my love!

>   SYLVIA
>   Thus with a kiss I die.

24   INT. RUGBY STREET - BEDROOM - NIGHT   24

Sylvia's head BANGS into frame, with Ted kissing her,
falling on top of her. He tears at her clothes. Around
them, bare floorboards, no furniture, a few piles of
books on the floor.

Their passion is huge, rapacious, furious, as if fuelled
by some insatiable hunger to get at the insides of the
other person, to merge with them, to crash into them, to
become entirely one.

Even Ted seems surprised that his sexual fury is matched
by Sylvia's. They roll and tumble as if in some deadly
struggle.

25   INT. RUGBY STREET - BEDROOM - NIGHT - LATER   25

Sylvia, wrapped in a sheet, stares at her face in the
rusty, broken mirror of a dresser which also serves as
Ted's desk. Her lips are swollen, a big bruise swelling
on her cheek. She feels it with her fingertips.

Her fingers move up to something else -- a SCAR on her
cheek. Not fresh. But red, angry.

Now she looks down at the riot of papers on Ted's desk.
Manuscripts, notes... but there is something underneath
them. She moves some of the papers aside to discover a
THICK RED VOLUME OF SHAKESPEARE.

It is covered with Ted's notes... a bramble of glosses
and underlinings. Sylvia's fingers brush over the words:
they seem like some kind of esoteric cabbala, the promise
of an entry to another kind of world entirely.

Behind her Ted enters from the bathroom, naked. Sylvia
watches him in the mirror. He places his hands on her
shoulders. Kisses her. Then, noticing the scar:

                    TED (CONT'D)
          What's this?

Sylvia turns away.

30A   EXT. CAMBRIDGE PUNT ON RIVER - DAWN - MOVING   30A

The river is shrouded in mist. A massive sun rises
through the bare trees, watermelon-orange, reflected in
the river, so that the sky is where the river should be
and the river is where the sky should be.

Ted pilots the boat, drinking beer from a bottle, as
Sylvia lies in the prow, enjoying the rhythm of the water
against her hand.. The day is grey, cold, but neither of
them seem to feel it.

                    TED
          You wouldn't do that if you knew.

                    SYLVIA
          Knew what?

                    TED
          What was down there.

                                        (CONTINUED)

Sylvia takes him seriously for a moment, then decides
he's kidding. She looks back to the water as if trying to
see what lay beneath.

                    TED (CONT'D)
          I once caught a thirty pound pike
          half a mile from here. Four and
          half feet long. Vicious
          bastard... got its teeth clamped
          onto my hand. Had to club it to
          death with a rock. They'll take
          anything, pike, chub, bream,
          eels, the odd moorhen. JESUS,
          WHAT'S THAT?

Sylvia leaps away from the water, screaming, as Ted rocks
the boat violently.

                    SYLVIA
          What? What?

But Ted can't answer, he's bent double with laughter.

Now Sylvia catches sight of something.

                    SYLVIA
          Look!

Ted follows her gaze. A HERD OF COWS, staring at them
with impassive, dumb brown eyes. One MOOS.

                    TED
          Very intelligent animals, cows,
          you know.

                    SYLVIA
          Really?

                    TED
              (nods)
          No-one gives them credit.

Sylvia grins, an idea.

                    SYLVIA
          What do you think they'd prefer?
          Milton or Chaucer.

                    TED
          Chaucer. Obviously.

Sylvia stands in the punt.

                                        (CONTINUED)

                      SYLVIA (CONT'D)
           Ladies, I give you THE WIFE OF
           BATH
               (recites)
           "Experience, though noon auctoritee
           Were in this world, is right ynogh for me
           To speke of wo that is in mariage;
           For, lordynges, sith I twelve yeer was of age,
           Thonked be God that is eterne on lyve,
           Housbondes at chirche dore I have had fyve..."

We stay with her, watching her recite as the river slides
past, the cows chewing interestedly, Ted watching her in
bemused love, SPIRES rising behind them.

32   INT. CAMBRIDGE - SYLVIA'S ROOM - NIGHT   32

Ted and Sylvia lie in bed. They have just made love. Ted
is tracing patterns on Sylvia's face with his fingers. He
comes to the scar on her cheek. Sylvia tenses, hating to
have it touched, but lets him. And then she can't bear
it, turns away

                      TED
           How did you get it? The scar.

A battle plays out on Sylvia's face. Eventually she
decides. She has to tell him. She rolls towards him.

                      SYLVIA
           I tried to kill myself.
               (in for a penny)
           Three years ago. I had it all
           planned out. I broke into the box
           where my mother kept her sleeping
           pills, and crept into the crawl-
           space under the house, where
           nobody ever went. I took the
           pills, and I went to sleep. I was
           there for days. They had no idea
           where I was. It was in all the
           Boston papers... my picture,
           everything.

                      TED
           What went wrong?

                      SYLVIA
           I took too many of the damn
           things. I puked them up. Three
           days later my mother and brother
           heard me groaning.
               (MORE)

32   CONTINUED:

                          SYLVIA (cont'd)
                    They went down into the basement
                    and pulled me out.

                          TED
                    Your cheek?

                          SYLVIA
                    I ripped it on the concrete while
                    I was out cold.

Ted touches it with his fingertips.

                          TED
                    A memento mori.

                          SYLVIA
                    Yes. A reminder of death...
                          (suddenly intense)
                    ...because I was dead, you know.
                    As good as. Only I rose again.
                    Like Lazarus. Lady Lazarus,
                    that's me. Risen from the grave.

32A   INT. PUB - NIGHT   32A

Ted, Sylvia, Boddy, Morecambe and Tom are playing DARTS
in a smoky local pub. Ted shows Sylvia how to hold the
dart, and she lets fly with a sort of savage energy, hits
a THREE. APPLAUSE from the onlookers.

Sylvia heads back to the little group as Ted takes her
place in front of the board.

                          BODDY
                    So what's the secret?

                          SYLVIA
                    What secret?

                          BODDY
                    Three months.

Sylvia, totally at sea.

                          MORECAMBE
                    It's a record. For Ted, anyway.
                    Normally he's a dent in the
                    pillow by day four.

                          BODDY
                    He lasted a week once. But she
                    lived two hundred miles away.

                                                    (CONTINUED)

                         MORECAMBE
               And didn't have a telephone.

     Now it's Sylvia's turn to throw again. She takes the
     darts and is about to throw, but again Ted takes her hand
     as if to show her how to throw. But instead he whispers
     in her ear.

                         TED
               Oh, my America! My new-found land.
               My kingdom, safeliest, when with one man man'd
               My mine of precious sones, my emperie
               How blest am in discovering thee!

     Now he leans even closer, and whispers something that
     even we can't hear. Boddy and Morecambe watching. They
     swap a glance. What the hell is going on?

     As Ted whispers, Sylvia's eyes widen.

                         TED
               Finish.

                         SYLVIA
               To enter in these bonds is to be free.

                         TED
               Then where my hand is set my seal shall be.

     His hand is still on hers, still holding the dart. They
     throw it together. It hits the BULLSEYE.

     32D   INT. ST. GEORGE OF THE CHIMNEY SWEEPS - DAY   32D

     A wizened VICAR confers with Ted (in threadbare corduroy
     jacket and National Service tie, shaking an umbrella),
     and Sylvia (in a pink-knit twinset).

     A VERGER in a brown cassock stands behind them at the
     door.

                         VICAR
               You have the ring? Good, good...
               and the license? Excellent. Now,
               your witnesses...?

                         TED
               Nobody said anything about
               witnesses.

     Impasse.

                                                    (CONTINUED)

32D   CONTINUED: 32D

                         SYLVIA
                    (re Verger)
               What about him?

                         VICAR
               You need two.

          Sylvia sags.

                         TED
                    Stay here.

          He runs out of the church.

          The three of them stand awkwardly by the altar.

                         VICAR
                    (to Sylvia, making
                    conversation)
               So how do you like England?

          Before Sylvia can answer Ted reappears, wet through,
          dragging a bedraggled and confused-looking PASSER BY with
          a shopping bag with him down the aisle.

                         TED
                    (to the man)
               You stand there.

          He takes his place by Sylvia.

                         TED
                    (to Vicar)
               Go ahead.

                         VICAR
                    (to the empty church)
               We are gathered here today to
               witness the joining together in
               matrimony of Edward James Hughes
               and Sylvia Plath...

35   INT. ST. GEORGE OF THE CHIMNEY SWEEPS - LATER   35

          Sylvia's eyes are bright with tears. They run down her
          cheeks as the Vicar continues (NB all dialog from the
          1665 Anglican Book of Common Prayer).

35 CONTINUED: 35

>   VICAR
> Eternal God, Creator and
> Preserver of all mankind, send
> thy blessing upon this man and
> this woman, so they may surely
> perform and keep the vow and
> covenant betwixt them made, and
> may ever remain in perfect love
> and peace together.

The vicar joins their hand together.

>   VICAR (CONT'D)
> Those whom God hath joined
> together let no man put asunder.

Sylvia and Ted KISS.

She holds Ted tight, as if to never let him go.

35C I/E. RUGBY STREET - KITCHEN/LIVING AREA - DAY 35C

Sylvia at the sink, cleaning BATTERED POTS AND PANS with a Puritan vigour. The kitchen around her has been transformed from something you might find into a shanty town into a reasonable facsimile of an ad from an American magazine.

Ted appears at the door.

>   TED
> Bloody hell.

>   SYLVIA
> What do you think?

>   TED
> You mean there was a kitchen in
> here the whole time?

41 INT. RUGBY STREET - BEDROOM - DAY   41

YACKATACKATATACKA-KACHING. Sylvia sits at the desk by the window, typing. Her fingers FLY. One corner of the room has been turned into a kind of makeshift office, and organised with the same ruthless efficiency that did for the kitchen.

Like the rest of the house, the living room has been transformed, swept clear of debris and now neatly arranged, even though the furniture is still horsehair and orangeboxes.

            (CONTINUED)

Beside her there's a THICK REFERENCE BOOK whose spine
reads 'INDEX TO GRANTS AND AWARDS'. Below it is 'WRITER'S
AND ARTISTS YEARBOOK 1957'.

On the wall above the desk, LETTERS and REJECTION SLIPS
have been neatly pinned. "Dear Mr Hughes... although your
work shows promise... Dear Mrs Hughes...we regret to
say... cannot offer you... please think of us in
future..."

SOUND of the front door, and men's voices. Ted enters,
carrying a bagful of books.

He heads over to Sylvia, kisses her. He inspects the wall
of rejections.

                    TED
          How many today?

                    SYLVIA
          Two. The manuscripts went
          straight back out. And I typed up
          four more complete copies of your
          book - so that's seven in
          circulation now.

                    TED
          Should have the house wallpapered
          by Christmas.
                    (picks up reference
                     book)
          Look, here's one we haven't
          applied for.
                    (as she cranes to see)
          There IS a Nobel prize for
          literature, isn't there?

Sylvia giggles, starts TYPING again.

41A   INT. RUGBY STREET - KITCHEN/LIVING AREA - LATER   41A

Sylvia, still typing. Tom and Ted are lounging around
drinking whiskey and listening to jazz.

                    TED
          Sylvia's old college has offered
          her a teaching job.

                    TOM
          I thought she loved England.

                                                    (CONTINUED)

41A   CONTINUED:

                              TED
                    She says everything's the same
                    shade of shit brown, and the
                    whole country's bogged down in
                    this warped feudal mentality.

                              SYLVIA
                         (YELLING from bedroom)
                    All the cars look like hearses,
                    no-one has a dentist, and the
                    food! Lard and stale bread
                    pudding garnished with cold pigs'
                    feet! Cow's tongue in aspic!
                    Sliced brains! Eel pie!

                              TOM
                    She's got a point.

                              TED
                    I know.

                              TOM
                    What would you do?

                              TED
                    I'm going to win a prize,
                    apparently, and publish a book
                    that will get the most amazing
                    reviews, and then everything will
                    be fine.

          Sylvia, still CLATTERING away on the keys.

                              TED
                    She's got it all worked out.

43A   INT. RUGBY STREET - KITCHEN/LIVING AREA - NIGHT   43A

          Ted and Sylvia sit together, listening to the jazz.
          CANDLES burn. They are both a bit drunk, judging from the
          empty wine bottle.

                              SYLVIA
                    Do you really think we'll make it
                    to America?

                              TED
                         (an idea)
                    Let's find out.

43A   CONTINUED: 43A

He gets up, grabs paper and a pen, and begins
methodically ripping up paper and writing the letters A-Z
and the numbers 1-9 on the pieces, then arranges them on
a semicircle on the kitchen table.

Sylvia, with her wine glass, watches him, amused.

                    TED
          Finish your wine.

Sylvia does, hands him the glass, which he sets in the
centre of the improvised Ouija board.

                    SYLVIA
          Now what?

Ted motions for her to sit down. She does.

                    TED
          Go on, it won't bite.

Sylvia touches the glass. Ted covers her hand with his.

                    SYLVIA
          What now?

                    TED
            (to the glass)
          Is there anybody there?

Sylvia GIGGLES. But now the glass slides over to YES.
Sylvia, suddenly spooked.

                    SYLVIA
          You made it do that.

                    TED
          His name is Pan.

An old friend, apparently.

                    TED
            (to the glass)
          We want to know if we're going to
          America, Pan.

The glass slides over to YES.

A look between Sylvia and Ted. Inter-resting!

                    TED
          You ask something.

Sylvia thinks for a moment then leans forward.

                                            (CONTINUED)

                       SYLVIA
            Is there anybody else there?

Ted's surprise at the question. Like who? But the glass
moves. 'YES'.

                       TED
            Who is it, Pan? Who's there with
            you?

The glass begins to move. It's spelling something out.

P-R-I-N-C-

                       TED
               (watching the glass)
            Prince... Otto.
               (amused)
            Hello, Otto.

But Sylvia isn't finding it funny. She's gone white,
remains silent.

                       TED
               (intrigued, to the
               glass)
            Who is he, Pan, Prince Otto?

The glass moves again, spelling --

                       TED
            B-I-E-N-E-N... Bienenkonig?
               (to Sylvia)
            It's German. Bee-king. King of
            the Bees. Something like that.

                       SYLVIA
               (oblivious, her voice
                not quite steady)
            Can I speak to him?

The glass slides to NO.

                       SYLVIA
               (upset)
            Why not, Pan? Does't he want to
            speak to me?

The glass doesn't move. Ted, watching Sylvia, registering
her distress, wondering what the hell all this is about.

                       TED
               (gently)
            Try something else.
                              (CONTINUED)

43A   CONTINUED: (3)   43A

                              SYLVIA
                    Where is he, Pan?
                         (sudden thought)
                    Is he here in the room with us?

The glass slides to YES. A chill goes down Ted's spine.
Sylvia looks around, frantic.

                              SYLVIA
                    Show me where he is!

A beat, then the glass slides abruptly not to YES or NO,
but to Ted.

Sylvia looks at Ted in shock, and then faster than either
of them can register, she smashes the glass. The pieces
cut her hand. She stares at the blood.

Ted, totally adrift, and more than a little shaken.

                              TED (CONT'D)
                    What's going on?

But at that moment a tear escapes from her eye, and
before she knows what is happening, she's crying.

Ted holds her in his big arms. The sobs rack her, harder
and harder. She seems to be dissolving away, becoming a
little girl.

43AaA   INT. RUGBY STREET - KITCHEN/LIVING AREA - LATER   43AaA

Sylvia has fallen asleep in ted's arms. The candles have
burned down. Ted's face, his questions unanswered.

43B   EXT. RUGBY STREET - EARLY MORNING   43B

A TELEGRAM BOY of about fifteen cycles along the early
morning street.

44   I/E. RUGBY STREET - HALLWAY - EARLY MORNING   44

Ted hair wild, in singlet and pants, opens the door.

                              TELEGRAM BOY
                    Telegram, sir.

Ted rips it open. His jaw drops.

                              TELEGRAM BOY (CONT'D)
                    Any reply, sir?

                                                    (CONTINUED)

44   CONTINUED: 44

                         TED
                    Fuck me.

                         TELEGRAM BOY
                    Very good, sir.

45   INT. RUGBY STREET - BEDROOM - DAY   45

Sylvia's still asleep, under the covers. THUNDER of Ted's
feet on the stairs.

                         TED (O.S.)
                    SYLVIA!!! SYLVIA!!!

He BURSTS in. Sylvia rouses herself, still half asleep.

                         TED (CONT'D)
                    I don't believe it!

                         SYLVIA
                    What time is it?

                         TED
                    Never mind the bloody time!

He brandishes the letter. Sylvia takes it, wipes sleep
from her eyes so she can read, props herself up.

                         SYLVIA
                    'OUR CONGRATULATIONS THAT HAWK IN
                    THE RAIN JUDGED WINNING VOLUME
                    POETRY CENTER FIRST PUBLICATION
                    AWARD'.
                         (to Ted)
                    You've won!

                         TED
                    I've fucking won!

The both start dancing on the bed, holding hands.

                         TED (CONT'D)
                    I've won! I've won!

                         SYLVIA
                    You've won! You've won!

                         TED
                    I didn't even know I'd entered.

Sylvia giggles. Slowly they stop, draw closer.

                                              (CONTINUED)

45   CONTINUED: 45

                         TED
               You know what this means, don't
               you?

                         SYLVIA
               You'll be a published poet.

                         TED
               And?

                         SYLVIA
               We're going to America?

     He nods. Her grin, as big as a watermelon.

                         TED
               And?

                         SYLVIA
                    (running out of
                     answers)
               Pan was right!

                         TED
               And?
                    (she has no idea)
               I'm going to fuck your brains
               out.

46   EXT. LINER - NEW YORK CITY - DAY - SUMMER   46

            SUPER: NEW YORK CITY, 1957

            Ted and Sylvia on deck, watching the STATUE OF LIBERTY
            slide past. Sylvia's crying, so glad to be home. Ted's
            arm around her, on the brink of a world full of
            possibility.

46aA   EXT. AURELIA'S HOUSE - BACK GARDEN - DAY   46aA

            A broad expanse of American lawn, a MARQUEE centre. WHITE
            COATED FLUNKEYS are laying out a big catered BUFFET,
            flapping starched white linen TABLECLOTHS over rickety
            TRESTLES, as a FLOWER ARRANGER makes adjustments to the
            TABLE DECORATIONS.

            Overseeing this is AURELIA PLATH. In her late fifties,
            wearing a tweedy twinset, her hair tightly controlled,
            and the air of a woman formerly used to servants.

46aA   CONTINUED: 46aA

She looks like a high ranking secretary at the UN, but in
fact she is an East Coast bluestocking, a kind of
intellectual soccer mom. She seems to be taking some grim
kind of pleasure in ordering the help around.

                    AURELIA
          Bring the tables together please.
          Now, the Gardenias, over there.
          No, not there. There. For
          heaven's sake!

                    SYLVIA (O.S.)
          Mummy!

Aurelia turns to see Sylvia rushing towards her, her hair
too up like a secretary. With her is Ted, loping behind.

Sylvia runs up and embraces her mother, who seems ill at
ease with such an overt show of affection.

                    SYLVIA (CONT'D)
          It's SO lovely to see you. How
          are you? You look wonderful! You
          hair's marvellous like that! And
          all this trouble! You shouldn't
          have!

                    AURELIA
          Welcome home, darling.
              (gently but firmly
               disengaging from the
               embrace)
          So this is the ubermensch?

Sylvia moves aside so that Aurelia can get a good look at
Ted, beaming proudly as Aurelia takes in the worn out
faded black corduroy jacket, the lank uncut hair.

Aurelia tries not to show her disappointment, and just
about resists the urge to inspect Ted's fingernails as he
reaches out to shake her hand.

                    TED
          Sylvia's told me a lot about you.

                    AURELIA
          Let's hope for both our sakes
          some of it was true.

46A   INT. AURELIA'S HOUSE - KITCHEN - DAY   46A

Sylvia and Aurelia are both furiously handwhisking
mayonnaise in bowls. Behind them is an array of cakes
which would shame a Patisserie, clearly all home made.
                                              (CONTINUED)

Aurelia slacks off in the mixing for a moment, giving
Sylvia the chance to ask:

> SYLVIA
> What do you think?

> AURELIA
> It's still be too runny.

She starts whisking again.

> SYLVIA
> About Ted.

Aurelia stops whisking. She looks through the kitchen
window. Ted is stalking about the garden, getting in the
way, picking at the piles of food and looking very
foreign. He's got a bottle of wine from somewhere.

> AURELIA
> He's very...

> SYLVIA
> What?

> AURELIA
> I don't know.

> SYLVIA
> Why can't you just be pleased for
> me for once?

You can tell instantly this is an old refrain between the
two of them.

> AURELIA
> How is he going to support you?

> SYLVIA
> I don't WANT to be supported.
>   (off her mother's
>   scepticism)
> He's going to be a great poet.
>   (more scepticism)
> I've got some money saved up.

> AURELIA
> And when that runs out?

> SYLVIA
> I'll teach, or write stupid
> stories for women's magazines.
> Does it matter?

                                            (CONTINUED)

                              AURELIA
                Darling, you know I've only ever
                wanted the best for you.

                              SYLVIA
                He IS the best for me.

                              AURELIA
                What do you want me to say?

                              SYLVIA
                That you like him.

Aurelia sighs, takes Sylvia's hand, peers at the gold
wedding ring. A fait accompli.

                              AURELIA
                Do you love him?

                              SYLVIA
                Yes, I love him.

                              AURELIA
                Then I like him.

52   EXT. AURELIA'S HOUSE - DAY - LATER   52

The party is in full swing now. Sylvia, with Ted by her
side, is working a WASPy crowd of ACADEMICS, LITERATI and
MIDDLE AGED WOMEN Aurelia has gathered together.

She looks perfectly at home in a twin-set like her
mother's. Ted out of place with his shabby austerity
clothes and uncut hair. He looks uncomfortable, and very
foreign.

                              SYLVIA
                Oh, Mrs. Bergstrom, how lovely to
                see you! Yes, this is Ted! Isn't
                he just? Mr. Van der Valk! How
                are you? And Cynthia? In
                Connecticut! Insurance! How
                fascinating!

Now Aurelia hoves into view.

                              AURELIA
                How are you enjoying yourselves?

                              SYLVIA
                All these lovely people. You've
                made us feel so at home! Hasn't
                she, Ted?

                                                          (CONTINUED)

                              TED
                        (very Northern)
               If I close my eyes I could be
               back home in Mitholmroyd.

She gives him a bit of a look, then to Sylvia.

                              AURELIA
               Your hem is crooked, dear.

Sylvia instantly squirms to straighten it. Ted, clocking
how she behaves in front of her mother.

Now Aurelia's attention is distracted by two passing
GOODWIVES.

                              AURELIA
               Martha! Elizabeth! Come and meet
               Ted!

                              ELIZABETH
                        (fanning herself)
               My, aren't <u>you</u> the catch of the
               day?

                              AURELIA
               Ted's going to be a great poet.
               His last book won the...

                              SYLVIA
                        (on cue)
               New York Poetry Centre prize.

Ted grits his teeth. This Sylvia is new to him.

                              AURELIA
               It's called THE HAWK IN THE RAIN.
               It's rather wonderful.

                              TED
                        (to Aurelia, surprised)
               You read it?

                              ELIZABETH
               Oh, listen to that accent!

Aurelia gives him an ambiguous look.

                              TED (cont'd)
               What did you think of the poem
               about the giraffe?

                                          (CONTINUED)

52   CONTINUED: (2)   52

                         AURELIA
                It doesn't have a poem about a
                giraffe.

                         ELIZABETH
                Say something else.

                         TED
                I need a drink.

53   INT. AURELIA'S HOUSE - DAY   53

Ted stands with his drink in the dark, cool interior, by
a wall of bookshelves. Outside the party is still in full
swing. He skims the titles. Poetry, some zoology, a
little classical history. But now something catches his
eye. A bound book whose spine reads: 'BUMBLEBEES -
Plath'. Ted pulls it off the shelf, flips to the title
page. It reads:

                        BUMBLEBEES
                     AND THEIR WAYS
                Otto E Plath, MA, MSc, PhD

                         AURELIA (O.S.)
                Sylvia's father.

Ted turns.

                         AURELIA (CONT'D)
                Bumblebees were his speciality.
                It was all he thought about.
                Before the war, back in Germany,
                his colleagues used to call him
                the Bienenkonig. It means...

                         TED
                King of the Bees.

                         AURELIA
                That was Otto. King of the bees.
                     (indicating the party)
                You must forgive my friends, Ted.
                They haven't had your advantages.

                         TED
                And what would they be?

                         AURELIA
                Having to fight for things you
                want.
                     (beat)
                     (MORE)

                                              (CONTINUED)

53   CONTINUED: 53

                              AURELIA (cont'd)
                    That's why she loves you, you
                    know. Sylvia, I mean. There
                    were... I don't mean to seem
                    disloyal... but there were a lot
                    of other boys. But she wasn't
                    scared of them. She rather
                    frightened them, I think. But
                    you... you're different. If
                    anything, you frighten her.
                    That's why she likes you.

                              TED
                    I'd never hurt her.

                              AURELIA
                    Perhaps not deliberately.
                         (eyes boring into him)
                    We found her right where you're
                    standing, you know. She was so
                    pale, so white. We thought she
                    was dead. Some people want to be
                    found. Sylvia didn't. She crept
                    into a hole and waited to die.
                         (beat)
                    I did my best for her, you know.
                    But it wasn't easy. She wasn't
                    easy. None of it's ever been
                    easy.

                              TED
                    Life isn't meant to be easy.

Aurelia stares at him coldly. A beat, then she hands Ted
the book. He takes it. She doesn't let go.

                              AURELIA
                    Be good to her. Always.

It is a command, not a request. Real steel. Then:

                              AURELIA
                    I got the two of you a little
                    present.

Ted, feeling the book in his hand.

58A   EXT. CAPE COD BEACH - DAY   58A

Sylvia's feet, in the margin of the water. She watches,
blank, as the ebb and flow of the washes over her feet.

Now the sand moves to reveal something. It's a hermit
crab shell, perfect and translucent.

                                                        (CONTINUED)

58A   CONTINUED: 58A

    She bends down to pick it up. Something about it troubles
    her. She drops it back into the water, turns to Ted, who
    stands behind her, in front of an IDYLLIC BEACH HOUSE.

                    SYLVIA
              Isn't it perfect? We'll go
              swimming in the mornings, and in
              the afternoons I'll write. I'll
              have half a novel by the time I
              start at Smith.

    Ted grins, and runs towards her. He picks her up and
    charges with her into the surf. Sylvia kicks and screams
    in mock terror, laughing.

    They bodysurf in the blue-green water, getting rolled and
    tumbled. Sylvia gets pushed down, and for a second we are
    with her UNDERWATER being tumbled, as if she had suddenly
    entered another dimension, and now --

    -- emerging SPLUTTERING from the waves.

    Ted helps her up, gets knocked down himself.

60   EXT. BEACH - DAY   60

    Ted and Sylvia sit, drying off.

                    SYLVIA
              We used to live by the ocean.
              When I was little, I mean.
              Before...
                    (beat)
              I guess she really does want me
              to be happy.

                    TED
              Are you?

                    SYLVIA
              The happiest I've ever been.

                    TED
              Don't say that.
                    (off her look)
              I mean. Think about it. One day
              in your life, you'll be the
              happiest you've ever been, or
              ever will be. Then what?

60A   INT. BEACH HOUSE - BEDROOM - NIGHT   60A

Sylvia is unpacking her and Ted's suitcases, hanging up clothes in a closet. As she unpacks Ted's, however, she lifts a sweater to discover the GREEN BOOK.

It hits her like a blow in the stomach, so hard she has to sit down on the edge of the bed.

She opens the book, then closes it rapidly as she hears Ted approaching, shoves it back under the sweater.

He pokes his head into the room.

              TED
      How hungry are you?

              SYLVIA
      Ravenous.

61   INT. BEACH HOUSE - DAY   61

Sylvia has a typewriter set up at the dining table. Everything is perfectly, neatly set out. Thesaurus, dictionary, pencils, blank paper, a spare ribbon.

Sylvia stares at the blank page. And stares.

61A   EXT. BEACH - DAY   61A

Ted, sea-fishing in the surf.

61B   INT. BEACH HOUSE - KITCHEN - DAY   61B

Sylvia, baking. She mixes CAKE MIX with a wooden spoon, displacing her frustrated energy into the eggs, sugar and flower that spill from the bowl all over the pages of the cookbook and her apron.

62   I/E. BEACH HOUSE - DAY - LATER   62

Ted heads up the sandy path with a rod and a couple of BIG FISH. Sylvia meets him at the door. She's is covered in flour. She kisses him. Ted dusts flour off his jacket.

              SYLVIA
    Wow! Look at those! Did you have
    fun? It's cooling down now but it
    was SO hot earlier. Look at me!
        (MORE)   (CONTINUED)

62   CONTINUED: 62

                              SYLVIA (cont'd)
                    I've been baking. Are you hungry?
                    I hope you're hungry! I baked a
                    poppyseed cake, two sponges and a
                    cream pie, only it went soggy in
                    the centre so I had to do
                    another, but that one was much
                    better!

Ted peers past her. A whole mountain of CAKES AND PIES
rests on the table. The typewriter and books have been
cleared neatly to one side.

                              SYLVIA (CONT'D)
                         (seeing his face)
                    Some men would be happy their
                    wives spent a a whole beautiful
                    sunny afternoon baking for them.

                              TED
                    I am happy.

                              SYLVIA
                    I've got the whole summer to
                    write.

63   EXT. COAST - DAY   63

Ted, a bag slung over his shoulder, wanders along the
ocean's edge, lost in thought. He stares out at the
ocean. Eventually he finds a rock, sits down, takes out a
notebook, and begins to write something.

63B   INT. COTTAGE - CAPE COD - DAY   63B

Sylvia sits at the typewriter. She pecks away at a few
keys. Then an idea briefly grabs her. She adds a couple
of sentences to the half a page of typing she's managed.
Then runs out of steam again.

63C   EXT. COTTAGE - CAPE COD - DAY - LATE AFTERNOON   63C

Ted heads up the sandy path. Sylvia meets him at the
door, kisses him.

                              SYLVIA
                    How was your walk?

                              TED
                    I got a poem, a good one. You?

She doesn't answer. Behind her, CAKES. Lots of them.

                                              (CONTINUED)

63C   CONTINUED:

                   SYLVIA
          I've dried up. I'm dry.

                   TED
                (teasing her)
          You've got nothing to say.

                   SYLVIA
          I'm not a real writer.

                   TED
          You never will be.

                   SYLVIA
          I'm no good!

                   TED
          But your cakes are excellent.

64   I/E. ROWING BOAT - OCEAN - DAY   64

Ted, rowing hard as he talks. Sylvia, at the prow,
staring into the green water as if it contained
mysteries. There is a slight tone of frustration in Ted's
voice, as if he were stating the obvious but Sylvia was
refusing to see it.

                   TED
          You know what your trouble is?

                   SYLVIA
          My husband thinks he can tell me
          how to write poetry.

                   TED
          There's no secret to it. You just
          have to take hold of a subject
          and shove your head into it.

                   SYLVIA
          That's easy for you to say. You
          go for a bike ride and come back
          with an epic in hexameters. I sit
          down to write and what do I get?
          A bake sale.

Ted grins. Now Sylvia becomes more serious.

                   SYLVIA
          My trouble is I don't <u>have</u> a
          subject.

(CONTINUED)

>   TED
>   Really?
>   (heaving on the oars)
>   'Falcon Yard'... the novel...
>   what's that about?
>
>   SYLVIA
>   A girl... who meets a boy...
>
>   TED
>   No, what's it really about?
>
>   SYLVIA
>   You and me.
>
>   TED
>   But, really...
>
>   SYLVIA
>   Me.
>
>   TED
>   The girl who spends the summer on
>   the beach...
>
>   SYLVIA
>   That's not me.
>
>   TED
>   Yes, it is. The family are the
>   Cantors. You told me.
>
>   SYLVIA
>   All right, all right. You're very
>   clever. I'm obsessed with myself.
>   So what?
>
>   TED
>   (a bit frustrated
>   again)
>   I'm just saying is, you already
>   have your bloody subject. Shit!

It takes Sylvia a moment to realise that he's not still
talking about her poetry.

>   TED
>   The wind's blowing us out.

They've left the river mouth behind now, and are just a
tiny boat in a great ocean, with dark clouds gathered on
the horizon. It's as if Ted had decided to row across the
Atlantic single-handed.

                                                    (CONTINUED)

64   CONTINUED: (2)   64

Ted is struggling to haul them around, working on one of
the oars. She sits up.

                    SYLVIA
            Can't you row back?

                    TED
            It's too strong.

He leans on the oars, starting to sweat. He looks
genuinely afraid. Sylvia on the other hand seems to be
almost enjoying the experience.

                    TED
                (he sounds worried)
            People drown like this.

                    SYLVIA
            Do they?

A strange tinge of anticipation, or satisfaction, in her
voice. Ted, picking it up, a little unnerved.

                    SYLVIA
            I tried to drown myself once. I
            swam out into the ocean, as far
            as I could, but the water spat me
            out like a cork. I guess it
            didn't want me.
                (to herself)
            Full fathom five, my father lies
            Of his bones are coral made
            Those are pearls, that were his
            eyes.

Ted, watching her, starting to have an inkling of what
all this is about, and sensing an opening.

                    TED
            Prince Otto.

Sylvia stares at him. For a moment it seems he might have
committed some terrible faux pas, but then her face
softens.

                    SYLVIA
            I was always happy. Until I was
            nine, that's all I can remember.
            Being happy and the sun shining
            and the waves crashing on the
            beach and my Daddy. Then one day
            he went off to hospital and never
            came back. It was just like he
            vanished. Or ran away.
                (MORE)   (CONTINUED)

64   CONTINUED: (3)   64

> SYLVIA (cont'd)
> And after that it was just me and
> mummy, and we moved away from the
> ocean and nothing was ever the
> same.

She starts to cry, despite herself.

> SYLVIA
> I just wanted to talk to him. I
> just wanted to talk to my Daddy.

> TED
> Nothing of him that doth fade,
> but has suffered a sea-change,
> into something rich and strange.

Sylvia stares at him, as if a crack had opened up in
reality. An epiphany, or an awakening.

Now there is the distant CHUG of a MARINE DIESEL. Ted
looks round to see a RUSTY BOSTON WHALER heading towards
them.

He stands in the boat, waves and YELLS.

65B   EXT. OCEAN - DAY   65B

The whaler tows them in towards the jetties of a small
harbour.

67   INT. BEACH HOUSE - BEDROOM - NIGHT   67

Ted sleeps, alone. The space beside him empty.

67A   INT. BEACH HOUSE - KITCHEN - NIGHT   67A

Sylvia moves through the main room. The moon burns bright
through the window. She still carries the same intensity
as in the boat. She wanders around the room like a ghost,
a spirit finding her body.

Eventually she goes to the table. The typewriter, the
bright white paper.

She sits, catches her face in the window. Outside the
ocean thunders.

(CONTINUED)

67A   CONTINUED: 67A

          She begins to type. Slowly at first, then accelerating
          unti she is HAMMERING the typewriter keys with an
          intensity and concentration we have not seen before.

          Beside her is the green BEE-BOOK.

          Now Ted appears at the door, bleary-eyed.

          Sylvia turns, sensing his presence, then goes back to the
          writing.

          Ted watches her.

          Her fingers HAMMER and HAMMER.

71   EXT. SMITH COLLEGE - DAY   71

          SUPER: SMITH COLLEGE, MASSACHUSETTS - 1957

          The big trees around the old brick buildings are tinged
          with fall colours.

72   INT. SMITH COLLEGE - LECTURE ROOM - DAY   72

          Sylvia is striding about in front of several ranks of
          rich, smart, young peppermint-scented STUDENTS. But she's
          taking no notice of them, lost in the spirit and energy
          of her own delivery.

                         SYLVIA
                    (loud, confident)
               What does the language of Henry
               James teach us? That life is rich
               and circuitous, that our every
               act and word carries great riches
               of implication and significance,
               and that therefore by studying
               them as we study the language of
               a novel...

          She looks up. Each girl is an image of perfection. Each
          more perfect than the last. The types her mother would
          approve of. You can almost feel the air suck out of her
          with a whoosh.

                         SYLVIA
                    (pulling it back
                     together, but without
                     quite the same energy)
               ...
                         (MORE)

                                                        (CONTINUED)

72   CONTINUED: 72
                          SYLVIA (cont'd)
                    we might discover that the
                    simplest things we perceive are
                    by their very quality, also the
                    most highly wrought.

76A   INT. HARVARD LECTURE HALL - NIGHT   76A

       The lecture hall is grand and old. An old-money
       intellectual audience, dotted with INTELLECTUALS and
       threadbare LITERARY TYPES, along with a sizeable
       cotillion of ATTRACTIVE YOUNG FEMALE STUDENTS and WELL
       DRESSED RICH WOMEN, hangs spellbound on Ted's words as he
       reads Yeats from the podium.

                          TED
                    The quarrel of the sparrows in the eaves,
                    The full round moon and the star-laden sky,
                    And the loud song of the ever-singing leaves,
                    Had hid away earth's old and weary cry.

       Now, creeping in from the back, looking dog-tired and
       tweedy and clutching an overflowing file, here's Sylvia.
       She looks around for a seat but the place is full,
       eventually tucks in at the end of a row where an ELDERLY
       MAN makes room for her.

                          TED
                       (he sees her)
                    And then you came with those red mournful lips,
                    And with you came the whole of the world's
                    tears,
                    And all the sorrows of her labouring ships,
                    And all the burden of her myriad years.

       Sylvia looks around. The women all around her are
       spellbound, a light in their eyes.

                          TED
                    And now the sparrows warring in the eaves,
                    The curd-pale moon, the white stars in the sky,
                    And the loud chaunting of the unquiet leaves
                    Are shaken with earth's old and weary cry.

       A beat of total SILENCE, then APPLAUSE, and no-one
       applauding harder than the women.

       Sylvia, a little disconcerted for a moment, then she too
       starts to applaud.

77   INT. HARVARD LECTURE HALL - NIGHT - LATER   77

       Ted and Sylvia, with glasses of wine. A KNOT OF WOMEN has
       gathered around Ted.
                                              (CONTINUED)

They are dressed to the nines, sleek and moneyed and
groomed, practically mobbing him. Sylvia, conscious that
her hair is straggly. She's having to try hard to enjoy
herself.

Ted too looks threadbare. There are holes in the elbows
of his jacket, and his fingernails are dirty.

> FIRST WOMAN
> Your voice... so powerful.

> TED
> What did you think of the <u>words</u>?

> FIRST WOMAN
> (going blank)
> The words?

Sylvia rolls her eyes.

> SECOND WOMAN
> When is your <u>next</u> book coming
> out, Mr Hughes?

> TED
> When I've written it.

A ripple of unctuous laughter from the harpies.

> SECOND WOMAN
> (to Sylvia)
> It must be wonderful for you to
> be married to such a great poet.

> SYLVIA
> Excuse me.

She turns away, bottling up the anger she can feel
boiling up inside her. Ted disengages from his fan club,
joins her. Sylvia manages a smile.

> SYLVIA
> Look, would you mind if we just
> go home?

> TED
> I have to thank Merwin for that
> review. And Len Baskin's here. I
> should say hello.
> (seeing her sag)
> You take the car. I'll get a cab.

Sylvia glances over at the harpies, unsure, then nods.

79   INT. ELM STREET APARTMENT - NIGHT   79

Syvlia enters, more exhausted than ever. She dumps the
CAR KEYS on a table, heads into the kitchen, fishes out
some leftovers from the fridge, looks for a clean plate,
but doesn't find one. Pulls a dirty one from a PILE OF
DISHES in the sink.

Pours a GLASS OF WINE from the remnants of a bottle which
she tries to dump in the garbage, only it's full of
coffee grounds and rotting banana skins. Her exhaustion
morphing into irritation.

Now picks it all up and heads into the living room, where
she dumps the food onto the table, by her typewriter,
sits down. Starts to leaf through some manuscripts. Just
then there's a RING on the doorbell.

81   INT. ELM STREET APARTMENT - HALLWAY - NIGHT   81

Sylvia opens the door. A pretty SEVENTEEN YEAR OLD GIRL,
pageboy haircut. She has a folder in her arms.

                    GIRL
          Is Mr. Hughes in?

                    SYLVIA
          What do you want?

                    GIRL
          He said he'd look at my poetry.
               (off Sylvia's silence)
          He said it would be okay.

Sylvia holds out her hand. The girl reluctantly hands
over the folder.

                    GIRL (CONT'D)
          I'm sorry if I disturbed you.

Sylvia closes the door without answering.

82   INT. ELM STREET APARTMENT - LIVING ROOM - NIGHT   82

Sylvia enters. She riffles through the poems as if
looking for something hidden in there. Nothing is. She
scans a couple of stanzas. She rolls her eyes -- it's
clearly doggerel -- and chucks the folder onto the sofa.

                                              (CONTINUED)

She heads back to the table with the typewriter. She sits
down, tries to type a few letters. But she can't
concentrate.

She looks at the clock. Ten PM. She bites her lip.

83   EXT. ELM STREET APARTMENT - NIGHT - LATER   83

A CAB pulls up. Ted emerges, a bit drunk. Pays.

84   INT. ELM STREET APARTMENT - LIVING ROOM - NIGHT   84

Ted lets himself in. It's dark. He turns the light on, to
discover Sylvia, sitting there at the dining table, with
the girl's poems in front of her.

                         TED
                    (off her silence)
               I'm sorry.

                         SYLVIA
               What for?

                         TED
               I don't know yet.

                         SYLVIA
               Who is she?

                         TED
               Who?

Sylvia pushes the poems forward. Ted picks them up,
glances at them, drops them back on the table casually.

                         TED
               Nobody. A student. She was at
               that creative writing class I
               talk to. She'd written all these
               poems. I took pity on her.
                    (off her silence)
               What's all this about?
                    (a dawning realisation)
               You think I'm fucking her?

                         SYLVIA
               Are you?

                         TED
               God, it's really getting to you,
               this place, isn't it?
                    (MORE)

                                              (CONTINUED)

84   CONTINUED: 84

> TED (cont'd)
> Bunch of dried up malicious old
> women all terrified their men
> might start getting a taste for
> fresh meat.
> (gets up)
> As a matter of fact I'm not
> fucking her. But don't worry, as
> soon as I do start fucking the
> students, you'll be the first to
> know.

He walks out.

85   INT. ELM STREET APARTMENT - KITCHEN - DAY   85

Sylvia, up early, cleaning the kitchen, as if by
scrubbing the sink and emptying the garbage she could put
their lives in order.

86   INT. ELM STREET APARTMENT - LIVING ROOM - MORNING   86

Ted, asleep on the sofa with a blanket pulled over him.
The remains of a bottle of whiskey on the floor.

> SYLVIA (O.S.)
> (bright and breezy)
> Good morning.

Ted pulls the blanket away from his face, blinks
painfully in the light, his head pounding from a
hangover.

Sylvia, an apron over her tweeds, stands in front of him
with a tray, on which is stacked a fantasy of a hangover
breakfast... waffles, sausage, bacon, eggs...

> SYLVIA
> There's fresh coffee, and I
> squeezed you some juice. Now, do
> you want white or brown toast...?

> TED
> Look... about last night...

> SYLVIA
> You were right. I'm letting this
> place get to me.

> TED
> No... it's not just you. It's me.
> I mean, it's getting to me as
> well.
> (pulls himself upright)
> (MORE)

                                                      (CONTINUED)

86   CONTINUED: 86

                         TED (cont'd)
                I can't write here. I'm
                suffocating. All anyone's
                interested in is TV and
                dishwashers and how much you're
                making and what kind of car you
                drive and...

He tails off, seeing the disappointment in her face.

                         TED
                I think we should go back to
                England.

                         SYLVIA
                And live on what?

                         TED
                We'll survive.

It doesn't sound like an answer to Sylvia.

                         SYLVIA
                I'm late. Meet me for lunch.

She heads out. Ted starts munching on toast.

87   INT. SMITH COLLEGE - LECTURE ROOM - DAY   87

Sylvia strides about in front of the clones, energised.

                         SYLVIA
                      (reading)
                "Destroy! Destroy! Destroy! hums
                the under-consciousness. Love and
                produce! Love and produce!
                cackles the upper consciousness.
                And the world hears only the love-
                and-produce cackle. Until such
                time as it will have to hear. The
                American has got to destroy! It
                is his destiny!"
                      (beat)
                D H Lawrence on Nathaniel
                Hawthorne. Discuss.

88   EXT. SMITH COLLEGE - DAY   88

Students are streaming out. Sylvia emerges from the grand
lecture building. Girls are criss-crossing the quad,
heading for their residences. But no sign of Ted.

She sits down on the bench and waits.

88   CONTINUED: 88

Gradually the girls thin out, until there is no-one but
Sylvia.

Realising Ted's not coming, Sylvia picks up her lecture
notes, starts to walk, thinking. Her route takes her down
a small road to --

89   EXT. SMITH COLLEGE - PARADISE POND ROAD - DAY   89

-- Paradise Pond.

Suddenly she freezes, as she sees something.

It's Ted, with a 'broad intense smile, eyes into the
uplifted doe-eyes' of an attractive girl, pageboy
haircut, bare legs under shorts, lipstick, basking in the
attention of this rugged English literary man.

It's the girl who brought round the assignment.

The girl catches sight of Sylvia, thirty yards away,
bearing down on them. She says something to Ted, touching
his arm, then RUNS in the opposite direction.

Ted turns, sees Sylvia, the thunder in her face.

91   INT. ELM STREET APARTMENT - LIVING ROOM/BATHROOM -   91
          EVENING

A GLASS SMASHES on a wall. Ted unducks. Sylvia, in a
pitch of rage. Outside the night is closing in, and it's
beginning to rain.

                    SYLVIA
               Who is she?

                    TED
               No-one!

Sylvia advances on him, threatening.

                    TED
               I don't even know her name.

It's exactly the wrong thing to say. She swings a punch.
Ted, reacting fast catches her hand.

                    TED
                 (full of threat)
               Go ahead. Try me.

                                              (CONTINUED)

He releases her hand, with a push that hints of his
strength. Sylvia, realising the violence he might be
capable of. She gives him a look full of loathing and
walks out of the room into the bathroom.

In the bathroom, Sylvia stares into the mirror.

SOUND of the door opening. She looks in the mirror, sees
Ted enter behind her.

                    TED
          Her name's Sheila. Or Sandra.
          Something like that. She spotted
          me walking up by Paradise Pond.
          That's all that happened.

                    SYLVIA
          Is she in love with you?

                    TED
          How the hell should I know?

                    SYLVIA
               (almost believing him)
          Why did she run?

                    TED
          She was... late or something.

He knows it sounds weak. Sylvia's anger boiling up.

                    SYLVIA
          God, you've made a fool out of
          me. Typing out your damned poems
          over and over again so that you
          can further your damned
          reputation, wasting my time
          teaching instead of writing all
          so that I can bask in your
          reflected glory! They should give
          me a fucking medal for services
          to Anglo-American poetry.

                    TED
          In order to win a medal for
          poetry you actually have to write
          some.

                    SYLVIA
          Oh, but I don't have time to
          write, do I? And why not? Because
          I'm using up my life teaching, so
          that YOU can run around screwing
          students!

                                        (CONTINUED)

91   CONTINUED: (2)   91

                         TED
               All right, I admit it. I fucked
               her. Forwards, and backwards and
               sideways. And you know what? It
               was great. It was glorious.
               Feeling that young body under my
               hands...

                         SYLVIA
               Stop!

                         TED
               ...how hard her nipples got when
               I rubbed them with my palms...

                         SYLVIA
                    (screaming, hands over
                     ears)
               STOP IT!

                         TED
               I thought that's what you wanted
               to hear.

A long beat. Sylvia stares at him, as if suddenly
realising a truth.

                         SYLVIA
               Maybe you didn't fuck her, but
               you did in your head.

She walks out. Ted hears the front door SLAM.

93   INT. ELM STREET APARTMENT - NIGHT   93

Ted wanders out of the bathroom into the empty apartment.
The silence is deafening. He picks up a book, can't read
it. Pours himself a scotch, can't drink it. Sits down,
stands up.

He goes to the window, pulls the curtain. Through the
teeming rain he can see --

94   I/E. CAR - OUTSIDE ELM STREET APARTMENT - NIGHT   94

-- Sylvia sitting in the car, her hands on the wheel,
staring ahead through the river of water running down the
windshield.

98   I/E. CAR - OUTSIDE ELM STREET APARTMENT - NIGHT   98

Sylvia's hands grip the steering wheel, as if trying to
will the car into motion.

Now she begins to cry. She tries to stop herself, but she
can't. Great sobs shake her. It is as if someone had
died.

She lowers her head to the steering wheel.

Her arms relax.

99A   INT. ELM STREET APARTMENT - NIGHT   99A

Ted sits at the dining table, his head in his hands.

SOUND of the front door makes him look up.

It's Sylvia, completely drenched.

                    SYLVIA
          Don't ever leave me.

                    TED
          Let's go home.

100   EXT. FITZROY SQUARE - DAWN - EARLY SPRING   100

A CHILD'S WAIL carries over the slate rooftops of NW1 --

SUPER: PRIMROSE HILL, LONDON, 1960

101   I/E. FITZROY SQUARE - BEDROOM - DAWN   101

-- as an ASIAN MIDWIFE delivers Sylvia of a BABY GIRL
(FRIEDA).

She hands the child to Ted, but instead of giving it
directly to Sylvia, Ted pulls apart the curtain to reveal
the SUN, rising over the rooftops of NORTH LONDON.

                    TED
               (to the child)
          You see that? That's the world.
               (hands her to Sylvia)
          She was born with the sun.

                    SYLVIA
          Oh God, she's perfect.

                                        (CONTINUED)

101   CONTINUED: 101

The child WAILS --

102   I/E. FITZROY SQUARE - DAY   102

-- and WAILS, just part of the cacophony in a cramped and
drab two-room apartment. Pots are RATTLING and BUBBLING
on the stove, steaming up the windows, and the SHIPPING
FORECAST is playing on the radio.

Sylvia is in the kitchen with the child on her hip,
simultaneously stirring gravy with a wooden spoon and
talking on the telephone, whose cord is stretched tight
from the living room, about a PIECE OF PAPER she has in
her hand.

Ted sits in the hallway, HAMMERING at a typewriter, which
sits on a wobbly card table in a kind of hutch under the
stairs where coats hang.

He has cotton-wool stuffed in his ears.

                    SYLVIA
               (on the telephone,
               yelling over the
               noise)
          Page forty, not fourteen. The
          third line, 'immaculate' has two
          Ms. Fifteenth line, there should
          be a comma after 'button'. Page
          forty-one...

Now the DOORBELL RINGS.

                    SYLVIA (CONT'D)
          TED! TED! CAN YOU GET THAT? TED!

                    TED
               (he can't hear because
               of the cotton wool)
          What?

Sylvia mimes 'someone at the door', badly.

                    SYLVIA
               (into the phone)
          ...line twenty, there's a typo in
          'Narcissus' and two spaces before
          'belly' where there should only
          be one.

                                           (CONTINUED)

The DOORBELL rings again. Ted hears it, and has to shove
the card table and typewriter aside in order to get to
the front door, which he YANKS open a few inches to
reveal a nice looking intellectual man in his thirties
whom we'll come to know as AL ALVAREZ.

>   TED
>   (yells)
>   WHO THE HELL ARE YOU?

>   ALVAREZ
>   (his hand through the
>   gap)
>   Alvarez.

>   TED
>   WHAT?

Alvarez points to his ears. Ted suddenly realises he
still has them stuffed with cotton wool. He tugs it out.

>   ALVAREZ
>   Al Alvarez. From the Observer?

>   SYLVIA
>   (still on phone)
>   Now, look, about the cover...

>   ALVAREZ
>   I... I thought we had an
>   appointment... but if it's not
>   convenient...

>   TED
>   I'm so sorry... come in...

Al squeezes through the gap.

>   SYLVIA
>   (clocking him, still on
>   the phone)
>   Well, _why_ don't I get a picture?

103   INT. FITZROY SQUARE - LIVING ROOM - DAY - LATER   103

Alvarez sits with Ted, a manuscript in front of him,
notebook out. Sylvia's still in the kitchen, still on the
phone.

> ALVAREZ
> THE HAWK IN THE RAIN, that was
> wonderful of course, but this
> shows.... I wonder... do you have
> any recent work I could see?

> TED
> Yes, yes, of course.

He heads out of the room.

> SYLVIA
> (on the phone)
> No, I'm sorry, you'll have to
> talk to my agent about that. Good
> bye.

She hangs up.

> SYLVIA
> We haven't been introduced. Mr
> Alvarez, isn't it?

> ALVAREZ
> Mrs. Hughes, I presume.

> SYLVIA
> Night Shift.

> ALVAREZ
> I beg your pardon?

> SYLVIA
> You ran it. In the Observer.

> ALVAREZ
> Night Shift. That was a good
> poem.

> SYLVIA
> I know. I wrote it.

> ALVAREZ
> You're Sylvia Plath?

> SYLVIA
> The Sylvia Plath. I've got a book
> coming out.

104   INT. LONDON CLUB - LAUNCH PARTY - NIGHT   104

CLOSE on the cover of a book: THE COLOSSUS by SYLVIA
PLATH.

A HAND takes one, and we move with it to see that it is one of a pile of twenty or thirty stacked on a trestle table in a London club.

Spotty ASSISTANT EDITORS and equally spotty JUNIOR LITERARY CORRESPONDENTS are gathered in knots around what can only be described as IT GIRLS.

Sylvia, looking fabulous in a sock-em-in-the-eye cocktail outfit, is talking excitedly with Alvarez and her publisher JAMES MICHIE, who's pointing out hacks.

> MICHIE
> That's Charlie Metheringham. He's the TLS. Robinson, Critical Quarterly. The one with the wild hair, he's from the Telegraph. And the chap with big ears is easy. He's The Listener.

Sylvia's only half-listening, because a little way off, Ted is surrounded by a circle of GOOD LOOKING FEMALE LITERARY ADMIRERS. She glares at him but he doesn't even notice.

> SYLVIA
> That's a good sign, isn't it? That they all came, I mean?

Mitchie and Alvarez swap a glance.

> MICHIE
> Don't get your hopes up.

> ALVAREZ
> There's no bigger glut of anything in the literary world than slim first volumes.

> MICHIE
> It's a tough game.

> ALVAREZ
> The toughest.

Sylvia's face fills with determination. She sees one of the journalists Michie pointed out (ROBINSON) head towards the exit without a copy of the book.

> SYLVIA
> Mr Robinson! Mr Robinson! Excuse me! You forgot this.

                         ROBINSON
                    (takes it)
               Oh, er... thanks.

                         SYLVIA
               Do you think you might
               be...reviewing it?

                         ROBINSON
               This? Shouldn't think so. We just
               got the new Pasternak, then
               Betjeman's out next week, and
               there's an E E Cummings in the
               pipeline. Not in the same league
               really, is she, this Sylvia...
               wossname.

                         SYLVIA
                    (dry as a bone)
               Plath.

                         ROBINSON
               Poor thing, can't be easy for
               her. Being married to that.

          He indicates Ted, still surrounded by a doughnut of
          female sycophants, then pats Syvlia on the bottom and
          hands back the book.

                         ROBINSON
               Still, good party. Thank your
               boss.

          But Sylvia doesn't even hear. She's watching Ted. All the
          women are LAUGHING at something he just said.

107   INT. FITZROY SQUARE - BEDROOM - DAY   107

          Bright early morning sunlight. NEWSPAPERS are spread out
          over their big double bed. Coffee on a tray. Both Sylvia
          and Ted are rummaging through the Sundays. Frieda is in
          bed too, having fun SCRUNCHING and RIPPING the
          newspapers.

                         TED
               Alvarez did you proud. Listen to
               this!
                    (reads)
               "Her poems rest secure in a mass
               of experience that is never quite
               brought out into daylight...blah
               blah...
                    (MORE)

                                            (CONTINUED)

107   CONTINUED: 107

                              TED (cont'd)
                    it is this sense of threat, as
                    though she were continually
                    menaced by something she could
                    see only out of the corner of her
                    eye, that gives her work it's
                    distinction."

He hand her the newspaper. She glances at it.

                              SYLVIA
                    What about the rest?
                         (off his silence)
                    One review.

                              TED
                    A good review. Look, it's hard.
                    You always knew it was going to
                    be hard. My first book...

                              SYLVIA
                         (sardonic imitation)
                    "...won prizes".

She gets up, plucks Frieda up from the bed.

Ted, wondering where the hell THAT came from.

112   INT. FITZROY SQUARE - LANDING - DAY   112

Ted is TAPPING away on the typewriter again, checking
something in the THICK BOUND SHAKESPEARE that we first
saw in Rugby Street. The PHONE rings. Ted goes for it,
but Sylvia gets there first, Frieda in her arms.

                              SYLVIA
                    Hello?

A WOMAN'S VOICE says something. Her face hardens.

                              SYLVIA
                         (handing Ted the phone)
                    For you.

Ted takes the phone. He doesn't realise it but Sylvia's
watching him closely as he talks.

                              TED
                    Hello? Oh, hello!
                         (to Sylvia)
                    The BBC.
                         (back to phone)
                    Yes, nice to talk to you too.

He settles down on the arm of a chair to talk.

113   INT. FITZROY SQUARE - KITCHEN - DAY   113

Ted, still on the arm of the chair. Sylvia's in the
kitchen, staring out of the window.

                    TED (O.S.)
          Okay, great. I'll see you there.
          Yeah, I'm looking forward to it
          too.

He hangs up, heads into the kitchen.

Sylvia doesn't look at him, CLATTERS away.

                    TED
          That was the BBC. Woman called
          Moira Doolan. You remember... I
          sent that idea for a children's
          radio series to her...

                    SYLVIA
          No.

                    TED
          She wants to have lunch. I think
          she likes it.

                    SYLVIA
          Short notice, isn't it?

Ted, not rising to the bait, picks his coat off a peg.

                    TED
          (kisses her on the
          cheek)
          See you later. Wish me luck.

The CLOCK says 12:30.

114   INT. FITZROY SQUARE - LIVING ROOM - LATE AFTERNOON   114

Frieda plays in her playpen. Sylvia, trying to write, but
her mind is elsewhere. She checks the clock... almost
five now.

117   INT. FITZROY SQUARE - NIGHT   117

Frieda WAILS in her crib. Sylvia stands at the window,
looking out, seemingly oblivious. Turns to the CLOCK.
Just gone seven. A moment of decision. She goes to the
phone, flips through an address book. Dials a number.
                                              (CONTINUED)

117   CONTINUED:

                              SYLVIA
                         (over the screams)
                    Hello? Is this the BBC? I want to
                    talk to Moira Doolan. In
                    Children's radio.

          An OPERATOR'S VOICE crackles, puts her through. The line
          rings, then answers. A WOMAN'S VOICE answers.

                              SYLVIA (CONT'D)
                    Is this Moira Doolan?
                         (beat)
                    How long ago did she leave?
                         (beat)
                    Did you actually see her leave?
                    Was anyone with her? Are you
                    sure? Well, perhaps you could
                    check with her secretary. Yes,
                    I'm trying to get in touch with
                    Mr Hughes. Yes, it's extremely
                    important. Are you sure he didn't
                    leave a message? My name is
                    Sylvia Plath Hughes. Let me leave
                    my telephone number... well, how
                    do you know he's not coming back?
                    Don't take that tone of voice
                    with me!

          The person at the other end hangs up.

          Sylvia thinks a moment, then goes over to Ted's card-
          table, Frieda still WAILING in the background. The NOISE
          building.

          She goes over to Ted's card table. Stares at the pile of
          manuscripts on Ted's card table. Leafs through. Typed
          pages, GALLEY proofs, emendations, notes, letters,
          CUTTINGS.

          She picks up a MANUSCRIPT poem. Her knuckles are white.

          Methodically, she begins to TEAR it into little pieces.

118   INT. FITZROY SQUARE - STAIRS - NIGHT   118

          -- Ted, coming up the stairs, a bit drunk. He emerges
          onto the landing, fumbles for his keys. Before he can
          find them, the door opens. Sylvia, calm. The CLOCK shows
          midnight.

                              TED
                    Sorry I'm late.

                                                          (CONTINUED)

He tries to kiss her. Sylvia dodges it.

>   SYLVIA
>   Where've you been?

>   TED
>   With that BBC woman...Moira...

>   SYLVIA
>   This whole time?

>   TED
>   She's nice. We got on.

Sylvia doesn't say anything. Ted follows her into the
flat and starts removing his coat.

>   TED
>   In fact I think she might
>   commission a whole series...

His voice tails off as he sees his work, his manuscripts,
all RIPPED TO SHREDS.

Ted picks through it, speechless.

Sylvia watches him, waiting for a reaction.

>   SYLVIA
>   I called the BBC. They said your
>   Moira left at five...

>   TED
>   We went to dinner.

>   SYLVIA
>   They said she left alone.
>   (quiet)
>   Who were you really with?

Ted, still holding it together, just.

>   TED
>   She had another meeting first. I
>   went to the British Library

>   SYLVIA
>   Not your gift, is it, darling?
>   Fiction. Who was she? One of
>   those harpies from the book
>   launch? Did she flatter you? Did
>   she tell you what a great poet
>   you were? Did that get you hard?

                                            (CONTINUED)

                              TED
                         (under his breath)
                    Bitch.

                              SYLVIA
                         (trying to provoke him)
                    How disappointing. The greatest
                    wordsmith of his generation, and
                    all he can come up with is
                    'bitch'. That's not going to get
                    the ladies wet, now, is it?

Ted turns towards her, his anger boiling over. Instantly
Sylvia picks up a WOODEN STOOL, brandishes it, her eyes
flashing with an equal fury.

                              SYLVIA
                         (his words)
                    Go ahead. Try me.

Ted makes a move, and Sylvia brings the stool CRASHING
DOWN on a piece of furniture, so that it SPLINTERS.

                              TED (CONT'D)
                    Marvellous! Go on! Maybe if you
                    put some of THAT into your book
                    you'd have got a couple of
                    reviews.

He's hit a nerve. Sylvia swings the stool at him,
crashing onto his head and shoulders.

For a second Ted staggers, dazed, and then the anger
rises in him, unstoppable. His face fills with a fury
that is black, homicidal. Sylvia, realizing she's pushed
him too far.

                              SYLVIA
                    No.

Too late. A blow CRASHES into her face.

Sylvia opens her eyes to find she's on the floor, blood
spilling out of her nose.

Ted, breathing hard, watches her crawl to the couch.

Realising what he's done, he moves towards her. But
Sylvia flinches in terror.

Sylvia watches him take his coat and leave.

121   EXT. REGENTS PARK - NIGHT   121

The night is turning foggy. The park is deserted. Ted
appears out of the mist, head down, collar up against the
chill. His stomach turns with the thought of what he just
did.

Out of nowhere, comes the AN EERIE HOWLING. Like a dog,
but more plaintive, more alien. Ted stops to listen.

                    MAN (V.O.)
               It's the wolves.

A thin, weasel-like man in a cloth cap and muffler.

                    MAN
               In Regent's Park, the zoo. They
               say they only howl like that when
               somebody dies.

                    TED
               Or something.

                    MAN
               Like animals, do you? Look at
               this.

He opens his jacket to reveal a tiny FOX CUB.

                    MAN (CONT'D)
               Yours for a pound.

Ted stares at the sharp nose, the gimlet eyes.

                    TED
               Where did you get him?

                    MAN
               Found him, didn't I?

Ted stares at the cub. Some strange communication.

                    TED
                    (he wants to, but)
               I can't.

                    MAN
               What's a pound to a man like you?

                    TED
               It's not the money. We're in a
               flat... there's no room...
                    (MORE)

                                        (CONTINUED)

121   CONTINUED:

                     TED (cont'd)
           they need space, foxes... my
           wife's got a new baby...

The words are stones in his mouth.

The man sneers, and starts to walk away.

                     TED
                (after him)
           What are you going to do with
           him? If you can't sell him?

                     MAN
           What do you think?

                     TED
           Look, I'll _give_ you a pound...

                     MAN
           Keep your money.

He hides the fox-cub again, disappears into the fog.

Ted, watching him disappear. He thinks for a moment, then
turns and walks back into the fog in the opposite
direction.

121B   INT. FITZROY SQUARE - BEDROOM - NIGHT   121B

Sylvia lies awake in the dark. The SOUND of the front
door unlocking, opening and closing. Ted enters, stands
in the door.

Sylvia stares at the wall instead. A massive gulf.

                     TED
           This city. It's poisoning us.

Sylvia's silence.

Ted sits on the bed. He touches Sylvia's shoulder. She
flinches away from him. Ted, wondering how the gap
between them can ever be bridged.

                     TED
                (sits on the bed)
           I love you.

A beat, then Sylvia turns to see his eyes.

                     SYLVIA
           Do you?

Ted nods.

                                  (CONTINUED)

121B   CONTINUED: 121B

She turns away again. Not satisfied.

                    TED
            (gets up, his anger
            exploding again)
        For God's sake, what more do you
        want from me?

                    SYLVIA
        To believe you.

122   I/E. FITZROY SQUARE - DAY   122

Ted is showing a young couple around the flat.

DAVID WEVILL is in his twenties, rather wispy. His wife
ASSIA is a little older, and beautiful under mascara and
silks.

She is a little older than Sylvia, shorter, dark where
Sylvia is blonde, European where she is American, and tan
where Sylvia is fair.

Even the voice is intriguing: husky and smoky, the accent
cut-glass Kensington underlaid with German/Jewish.

A palpable hit of sexual attraction between Assia and Ted
as they move around the cramped flat. Ted, allowing
himself to enjoy it just a little on the grounds that he
will never see this delicious woman again.

                    TED
        So this is the bedroom...... the
        bathroom... the kitchen... the
        meters are here, under the
        stairs... and the living room
        you've already seen.

They end up in the living room with Sylvia, who has
Frieda on her hip. Ted brushes past Sylvia, who avoids
him. Their physical intimacy, replaced by awkwardness.

                    TED
        There's not much to it, I'm
        afraid, but...

                    ASSIA WEVILL
        No, no, it's beautiful. And it
        would be perfect for David.

                    SYLVIA
            (to David)
        Why, what is it you do?

                                                        (CONTINUED)

122   CONTINUED: 122

                              DAVID WEVILL
                    I'm a poet.

                              SYLVIA
                    So are we.

                              DAVID
                    You're...?

                              TED
                    Ted Hughes.

                              SYLVIA
                    ... and Sylvia Plath.

                              DAVID
                         (amazed)
                    I gave Assia your book. THE
                    COLOSSUS.

                              ASSIA
                    Your poems... they are very
                    beautiful. And very frightening.
                         (seeing Sylvia smile)
                    What?

                              SYLVIA
                    That's the best review I've ever
                    had.

          POP of a CORK as --

123C   INT. FITZROY SQUARE - LIVING ROOM - MINUTES LATER   123C

          -- Ted breaks open a bottle of wine in the kitchen, David
          at his shoulder.

          Through the doorway, Assia sits with Sylvia, engrossed in
          conversation. They talk with the intensity of new best
          friends. It is as if Ted's attraction to her is shared by
          Sylvia.

                              TED
                    I've been thinking about doing
                    some hendecasyllabics.

                              DAVID
                    Hendecasyllabics?

                              TED
                    "In the month of the long decline of roses
                    I, beholding the summer dead before me
                    Set my face to the sea, and journeyed silent".
                                               (CONTINUED)

123C   CONTINUED: 123C

                              (beat)
                    Swinburne. Loved them. But
                    they're damn tough. Try one.
                    Wait, I'll go first.
                              (thinks, then)
                    "This wine shall be a testament
                    of friendship"

He hands a glass to David, who takes it.

                         DAVID
                    Very good.
                              (enormous
                               concentration)
                    "Why won't everyone see the
                    flaming oyster".
                              (off Ted's laughter)
                    My God, I see what you mean.

                         TED
                    He also insisted on being flogged
                    regularly.

                         DAVID
                    Who?

                         TED
                    Swinburne.

                         DAVID
                    Suddenly it all makes sense.

Ted grins. A beat as the two men look over to the
continuing conversation between Sylvia and Assia. Ted,
taking in the curve of Assia's neck, the mascara, the
silks.

                         TED
                    Your wife... she's very
                    beautiful.

Assia, conscious of being watched.

                         DAVID
                              (pleased)
                    Yes, she is, isn't she?

At the table:

                         SYLVIA
                    Your father was German? Mine too.

                         ASSIA
                              (chain smoking)
                    Jewish German.
                              (MORE)   (CONTINUED)

123C CONTINUED: (2) 123C

> ASSIA (cont'd)
> But of Russian origin. We fled in
> thirty-eight, just in time.
> Sometimes survival is a matter of
> pure chance, don't you think?

Sylvia looks down. Too close to the bone.

> ASSIA WEVILL
> After that, we moved to
> Palestine, then Canada. That's
> where I got married.

> SYLVIA
> To David?

> ASSIA
> (snorts)
> God, no. Some Canadian. I can't
> even remember his name. After
> that there was a Professor of
> Economics, but he was no bloody
> use either.

> SYLVIA
> And David?

> ASSIA
> He's nice. You know.

Assia looks up, sees Ted, who's in the kitchen with
David, looking at her. Holds his gaze for just a fraction
of a second.

> SYLVIA
> You make him sound like a cup of
> tea.

> ASSIA
> Well, you know how it is.
> Sometimes you really fancy a nice
> cup of tea.

Sylvia giggles. Assia glances over to the kitchen. Ted is
looking at her again.

In the kitchen:

> DAVID
> You don't think it'll be
> isolating?
> (off Ted's distraction)
> Devon, I mean.

> TED
> It's _meant_ to be.

(CONTINUED)

123C   CONTINUED: (3)   123C

123D   INT. FITZROY SQUARE - NIGHT - LATER   123D

            Assia and David are putting on their coats.

                        DAVID
                        (to Ted)
                  Well, it's been wonderful to meet
                  you both. Thank you so much. Do
                  you think you'll be up in London
                  much?

                        TED
                        (conscious of Assia)
                  I don't know. I mean... I havent
                  thought about it... I don't think
                  so...

                        SYLVIA
                  Mustn't they?

            Ted jumps as he realises Sylvia, with Assia, is talking
            to him.

                        TED
                  What?

                        SYLVIA
                  Come to see us. David and Assia.
                  In Devon.

                        TED
                  Yes. Yes, I mean, sure.

            His eyes meet Assia's. Some communication there.

                        SYLVIA
                        (to Assia)
                  You will come, won't you?

                        ASSIA
                  We'd love to.

            She smiles.

124   EXT. DEVON COUNTRYSIDE - DAY - WINTER   124

            SUPER: DEVON, 1962

                                                      (CONTINUED)

124   CONTINUED: 124

          Gunnmetal clouds scud over a bleak moorland landscape, in
          the middle of which sits an IDYLLIC COTTAGE, like an
          outpost of domesticity in a sea of wildness.

          Now we pick up Ted, striding across the moor towards the
          house, looking like a poacher, or Heathcliff.

          This begins a MONTAGE SEQUENCE:

124A   INT. COURT GREEN - DAY   124A

          Sylvia feeds a THREE MONTH OLD BABY (Nick), sitting on a
          sofa with Frieda. Ted enters, fresh from the moor, hair
          wild. He smiles, sits down to play with the kids.

124B   INT. COURT GREEN - STUDY - DAY   124B

          Ted writes, longhand, his copy of Shakespeare visible
          beneath a sea of papers and notes.

124C   INT. COURT GREEN - KITCHEN/LIVING AREA - NIGHT   124C

          Ted, on a stepladder, trying desperately to mend a
          LEAKING ROOF, watched by Sylvia and Frieda.

124D   INT. COURT GREEN - KITCHEN/LIVING AREA - NIGHT   124D

          Sylvia sits at a typewriter, placed on the dining room
          table, Nick in her arms, using her free hand to peck at
          the keys. Ted brings her a cup of coffee.

124E   EXT. COURT GREEN - DAY   124E

          Ted and Frieda walk and play among the trees in the
          garden. (Maybe Sylvia watches from inside, still holding
          Nick).

          (In all of this a slight edge of tension that undercuts
          the apparently idyllic images. They are trying hard to
          keep afloat, but under the surface you sense there is a
          weight still capable of dragging them under. It's very
          subtle, just a matter of tone, but it's there)

          MONTAGE ENDS with:

125AC   INT. OUTBUILDING - DAY   125AC

Ted hacks and hews at a great PIECE OF WOOD on a makeshift workbench, covered in sawdust, pouring his feelings into a physical object.

He stops, inspects his work. It's finished.

125C   INT. COURT GREEN - LIVING AREA - DAY   125C

Sylvia watches Ted angle the huge piece of wood through the door.

               SYLVIA
      What the hell is that?

125D   INT. COURT GREEN - CONSERVATORY - DAY   125D

Ted heaves the slab of wood onto a pair of CARPENTER'S HORSES placed by a window to make table legs. Sylvia, watching.

               TED
      I thought...if you had a writing
      table...

He gets the desk set up. Sylvia goes over, inspects it. Through the window is a great tree, a great WYCH-ELM moving in the night wind. She runs her hand over the wood of the desk, one edge of which is unfinished bark, suddenly touched by Ted's effort.

               SYLVIA
        (feeling the bark)
      What is it? This wood.

               TED
        (a beat)
      Coffin Elm. It doesn't rot. So
      they use it for coffins. Keeps
      the dead looking good.

Sylvia smiles.

               SYLVIA
      It's beautiful.

               TED
        (beat, then)
      I have to go up to London.

                              (CONTINUED)

125D   CONTINUED: 125D

                          SYLVIA
              Why?

                          TED
              To meet people. So I can sell
              books and earn money.
                   (off her look)
              So we can buy food. And mend the
              roof. And not freeze to death.

125E   EXT. COURT GREEN - LATE AFTERNOON   125E

         Sylvia, with Nick in her arms, watches their car rattle
         away down the drive, taking Ted away.

         The noise of the engine DIES away.

         You suddenly realise how isolated the house is.

125F   INT. COURT GREEN - NIGHT   125F

         It's late. Sylvia checks on the children, asleep.

         She wanders the house like a ghost.

         She sits at the desk of coffin elm, stares out of the
         window.

         It's as if she doesn't know how to be alone.

125G   INT. COURT GREEN - BOOKSHELF - NIGHT   125G

         Sylvia runs her hands along the spines of the books,
         looking for something.

         Her fingers stop on the spine of a GREEN BOOK.

         The title: BUMBLEBEES - PLATH.

125H   EXT. COURT GREEN - DAY   125H

         The Morris rattles back up the drive, stops. Ted gets
         out, pulls out his suitcase, stops as he sees something.
         His surprise.

126   EXT. COURT GREEN - BEEHIVE - DAY   126

Sylvia, dressed in full beekeeping regalia, lifts SLATS
OF BEES from a SQUARE WOODEN BOX and inserts them into
the slots of a white painted HIVE. Bees BUZZ around her
like familiars. She looks like some high priestess of the
Bee-Cult. A bride, or a samurai.

Ted, approaching behind her, watching.

A BEE buzzes him. He swats it away.

                    TED
          Why don't they sting you?

                    SYLVIA
          I think they know.

                    TED
          Know what?

                    SYLVIA
          That I'm a beekeeper's daughter.

126B   INT. COURT GREEN - BEDROOM - NIGHT   126B

Ted and Sylvia, in bed together. Outside, the sound of
the restless trees moving in the wind. Neither of them
are asleep.

                    TED
          I saw David. Wevill. While I was
          up in London. He was at the BBC,
          doing a reading. I invited them
          down next weekend. Him and his
          wife. What's her name.

Sylvia's antenna, twitching. He knows perfectly well what
her name is. It's as if he's embarassed to say it.

                    SYLVIA
          Assia.

                    TED
          That's it, Assia.
                (picking something up)
          You don't mind, do you? I mean, I
          thought you wanted them to come.
          That's what you said, anyway.
          Isn't it?

126C   EXT. MOOR - DAY   126C

Assia and David are visiting, out for a walk with Ted and
Sylvia on the great barren expanse of moorland. Sylvia
and Assia walk together, close as sisters, or lovers.
Sylvia has on sensible shoes, Assia a pair of HIGH HEELS,
which make walking difficult as she picks her way through
the cowpats.

She has to reach out for support to Sylvia as she totters
through the mud.

                    ASSIA
          God, it's beautiful up here.

                    SYLVIA
          Some people think it's bleak.

                    ASSIA
          Not me.

                    SYLVIA
          Or me.

                    ASSIA
          It's so good to see you again.
          And Ted.
                    (beat)
          Isn't it funny?

                    SYLVIA
          What?

                    ASSIA
          How we share the same tastes.

Sylvia, suddenly picking something up.

Up ahead is a stile. Ted climbs over, to join David who's
already the other side. Asssia is next, but she finds it
hard in her high heels. She holds out her hand for Ted to
help her. He hesitates.

                    ASSIA
          Would you mind?

Ted puts out his hand. She takes it, jumps down. Passes
close to him. A smile.

                    ASSIA
          Thank you.

The smile is delicious. Sylvia sees it from behind.

126CA   INT. COURT GREEN - LIVING AREA - NIGHT   126CA

The four of them sit round a dinner table, laid out with
Sylvia's usual attention to detail. A TUREEN of soup in
the centre. They are halfway through the soup and a
bottle of wine down already.

                    ASSIA
          Such a house! A real poet's
          house. You must both be very
          happy.

She glances at Ted.

                    SYLVIA
          We've never been happier.
                    (to Ted)
          Have we?

                    TED
          No.

                    ASSIA
          This soup is extraordinary.

                    SYLVIA
          Have some more.

                    ASSIA
          Oh, no. Well, perhaps a little.
          Aren't I greedy? I've always been
          greedy.

Said with a little glance at Ted that Sylvia sees. The
maggot gnaws away in Sylvia's brain.

                    DAVID
          Ted says you have the new Robert
          Lowell recording.

                    SYLVIA
          What?

                    DAVID
          The new Robert Lowell recording.

                    SYLVIA
          What about it?

                    DAVID
          Perhaps we could listen to it
          later.

                                        (CONTINUED)

                    SYLVIA
          Yes, yes... of course.

She stands up abruptly, and starts gathering up soup
plates, although no-one has finished.

                    SYLVIA
          Thank you, thank you. Thank you.

She heads into the kitchen.

An awkward beat.

                    TED
               (gets up too)
          Excuse me.

He follows Sylvia into the kitchen.

David and Assia are only feet away. Ted HISSES so as not
to be heard.

                    TED
          What the hell is wrong with you?
          They're our guests, for Christ's
          sake!

                    SYLVIA
               (furious)
          Is that why she thinks she can
          help herself to everything that's
          mine?

Said loud enough for the Wevills to hear.

                    TED
          What the hell?

                    SYLVIA
          I've seen the way you look at
          her. Don't think I haven't.

                    TED
          You're imagining things.

                    SYLVIA
          Oh, am I? Well, if you think for
          one second I'm going to let you
          humiliate me...

                    TED
          Sylvia. No-one's trying to
          humiliate you.

                                        (CONTINUED)

He sounds calm, believable. For a moment, the wind goes
out of Sylvia's sails. She almost relents. But then:

                    TED
          I mean, why bother? You're doing
          such a good job of it yourself.

He turns and walks back to the dinner table, leaving her
standing there.

Sylvia, the heat of her anger turning to coldness.

Ted sits down at the dinner table again.

                    TED
          I'm sorry about that.

Now Sylvia again appears from the kitchen with the
perfect food, places it on the table.

She has a brittle smile, as if resolved to be pleasant.

                    ASSIA
          My God, look at this! You
          shouldn't have gone to all of
          this trouble.

                    SYLVIA
                 (dumping out food)
          Yes, I'm beginning to think that
          myself.

                    TED
          For God's sake!

                    SYLVIA
                 (pleasantly)
          How is everything?

                    DAVID
          Oh, delicious. Mmm.

                    SYLVIA
                 (to Assia)
          You're not eating.

                    ASSIA
          I -- I'm not hungry any more.

                    SYLVIA
          I shall be most insulted if you
          don't eat.

(CONTINUED)

She fixes Assia with a Gorgon stare. A beat, then Assia
takes a little morsel on her fork and eats it.

> DAVID
> (rather desperate)
> So... are you managing to write
> at all, with the baby?

> SYLVIA
> (deadly sweetness)
> Oh, me? No. But Ted is. And
> that's what really matters, isn't
> it? I mean, he's the poet in the
> family.

130   INT. COURT GREEN - LIVING AREA - NIGHT   130

The four of them sit uneasily in easy chairs, wine
glasses and dessert plates scattered round. Ted's anger
is still simmering. Assia is smoking, her resentment at
being humiliated clear. David has his hands pressed
together, eyes closed, head back, as if he has retreated
into the poetry, which Sylvia seems to be enjoying with a
kind of grim satisfaction.

> [They listen to Robert Lowell's recording of
> his poem "The Quaker Graveyard in Nantucket"]

Ted can't take it any more. He stands.

> TED
> I'll do the washing up.

Assia, suddenly seeing her opportunity.

> ASSIA
> (gets up)
> I'll help you.

Ted's alarm. He glances at Sylvia, whose fierce stare
tells you everything.

> TED
> No, it's okay. You stay.

> ASSIA
> I absolutely insist.

She gathers up a token plate and glass and disappears
into the kitchen with Ted.

Sylvia, suddenly sensing the situation slipping away from
her.

                                              (CONTINUED)

130   CONTINUED: 130

She glances over to David, who is either oblivious to
what is going on or has made a political decision to stay
out of it.

Sylvia rises.

130A   INT. KITCHEN - NIGHT   130A

Assia is at the sink, doing the dishes. Ted is drying up.
They are just a fraction too close together, talking in
low voices about something.

                    SYLVIA
            What's going on?

Ted has no words. Assia smiles at Sylvia, an insult of a
smile. David appears behind Sylvia, sensing that events
have finally reached a crisis.

                    DAVID
            Can I help with anything?

                    SYLVIA
            I'd like you and Assia to leave
            first thing in the morning.

                    DAVID
            But...

                    SYLVIA
              (finally snapping,
               almost crying)
            It's too much. I'm very tired.
            I'm exhausted, if you want to
            know. You don't know what it's
            been like. I've two young
            children. If you had children of
            your own you'd know what it's
            like.

Her anguish, totally naked.

                    DAVID
              (beat, then)
            I'm sorry. Of course.

133   INT. COURT GREEN - BEDROOM - NIGHT   133

Dead of night. The silent hour.

Sylvia, asleep. She murmurs something we cannot make out.

Ted, lying awake. His insides churning.

                                              (CONTINUED)

133   CONTINUED:

He sits up, swings his legs off the bed. Sits there a
moment in the half-light.

134   INT. COURT GREEN - KITCHEN - NIGHT   134

Ted pads into the kitchen, in pyjamas. He pours a glass
of milk from the fridge, sits down to drink it.

His face is a whole world of trouble. But now:

                    ASSIA WEVILL
          You couldn't sleep either.

He looks up. Assia, in a loose champagne-colored
nightdress of silk and lace.

She moves towards him. Ted, frozen.

In a single move, she pulls her nightdress up, revealing
she's naked underneath, and slips it over his head, so
they are both enveloped.

138   EXT. COURT GREEN - DAY   138

Ted throws a battered suitcase into the back of the
Morris Oxford. Sylvia watches him, Nick in her arms,
Frieda clinging to her leg.

                    SYLVIA
          When will you be back?

                    TED
          Couple of days.
               (slams the back door
               shut)
          Three maybe. Depends how it goes.
          I don't know.

                    SYLVIA
          What number will you be at?

                    TED
          Haven't decided who to stay with
          yet...I mean, the thing is... I
          think everyone's getting a bit
          sick of having me on their floor.
          I might just check into a bed and
          breakfast.

The lies fall like stones.

                                             (CONTINUED)

138   CONTINUED: 138

                         SYLVIA
                You don't have to go, you know.

                         TED
                Yes I do.

He kisses her, gets in the car.

Sylvia watches him drive off. Her face. The thing she has
most feared, coming absolutely true.

The RAZZ of the Morris engine turning to:

138B   EXT. COURT GREEN - DAY   138B

-- the BUZZING of bees.

Sylvia, in her priestess gear, pulls the top off a hive.
Bees swarm out, clambering all over her, on her mask
everywhere. The BUZZING of the bees, like a thousand
voices, suddenly turning to --

138C   INT. COURT GREEN - TED'S STUDY - DAY   138C

-- SILENCE. Sylvia enters, in beekeeping garb. The study
is a real writer's office, thick with books and papers
and letters.

On the desk is the RED SHAKESPEARE, open at a page.

Ted's handwriting, spidered over the page.

138CA   INT. SEEDY HOTEL - DUSK   138CA

Ted, climbing unfamiliar stairs to an unfamiliar door. He
hesitates, then KNOCKS.

138CB   EXT. COURT GREEN - GARDEN - AFTERNOON   138CB

Sylvia hauls dead bushes and branches across the garden
with a grim energy, piles them into the beginnings of a
BONFIRE.

138CC   INT. SEEDY HOTEL ROOM - DUSK   138CC

Ted and Assia make love, writhing and coiling. An ORANGE
SUNSET illuminates the room. They come together.

138D   EXT. COURT GREEN - GARDEN - DUSK   138D

A BONFIRE burns. Sylvia, silhouetted by the leaping flames, heaves PAPERS, LETTERS, PHOTOGRAPHS, CLOTHES onto it, a funeral pyre of their life together.

The RED SHAKESPEARE, burning.

138DA   INT. SEEDY HOTEL ROOM - DUSK   138DA

Ted and Assia come together.

138H   EXT. COURT GREEN - GARDEN - DUSK   138H

The bonfire has burnt down. Sylvia stares at the embers, orange glowing in her eyes. She pokes the ashes with a stick. Black, burnt FRAGMENTS OF PAPER rise like birds. One lands at her feet. She bends to pick it up.

On it is written A SINGLE WORD. We can't quite read it.

146   EXT. COURT GREEN - DAY   146

The Morris CRUNCHES to a halt in front of the house.

147   INT. COURT GREEN - HALLWAY - DAY   147

Ted enters.

                TED
          Hello? Hello?

No answer. He heads into --

148   INT. COURT GREEN - TED'S STUDY - DAY   148

-- and stops. The room is completely bare.

On his desk is a burned fragment of paper.

            SYLVIA (O.S.)
       The truth comes to me.

Ted turns. Sylvia, in the doorway. Out of the window, he notices the bonfire, still smoking a day later.

             SYLVIA
       The truth loves me.

                        (CONTINUED)

148   CONTINUED: 148

At that moment the PHONE rings downstairs. Their eyes
meet. Each of them knows who it is.

150   INT. COURT GREEN - FOOT OF STAIRS - DAY   150

SOUND of feet THUNDERING down the stairs, but then Ted
loses his footing and falls BANG BANG BANG all the way
down to the hallway, knocking the wind out of him.

Sylvia steps over him, picks up the BLACK TELEPHONE.

                    SYLVIA
          Hello?
                 (silence)
          I know who you are.

She hands the phone to Ted, who's on his feet. Ted takes
it, not knowing what she's up to.

                    TED
          Hello?

Sylvia YANKS the wire from the wall.

                    SYLVIA
          No more lies.

151   INT. COURT GREEN - HALLWAY - DAY   151

Ted has an OVERNIGHT bag. The door is open, a taxi behind
him. Frieda hangs on Sylvia's leg.

                    TED
          Look...

He tails off. There is nothing he can say that makes any
difference to anything, and he knows it.

                    SYLVIA
          I thought you were a God. I made
          you into my God. But you're not.
          You're just a man. My God, look
          at you. You're hardly even that.

She closes the door on him.

151A   EXT. AL ALVAREZ' FLAT - NIGHT   151A

A KNOCK at the door. Al answers it. It's Ted, with a
suitcase, soaked to the skin. He looks ragged, ashen.

                                              (CONTINUED)

151A   CONTINUED: 151A

                         ALVAREZ
              I'm not taking sides.

                         TED
              Just for a few nights. Please.

         Al lets him in.

152A   INT. COURT GREEN - BEDROOM - NIGHT   152A

         Sylvia lies, curled up like a fetus, hugging a pillow,
         rocking gently, despair in her sleepless eyes.

155   I/E. COURT GREEN - DOWNSTAIRS - DAY   155

         The front door is open, the Morris parked outside with
         doors open. Nick's already in there. Sylvia emerges from
         the kitchen carrying a packed lunch, followed by Frieda.

                         SYLVIA
              Come on! We're going to the
              seaside!

                         FRIEDA
              Don't want to.

                         SYLVIA
              Yes, you do. You'll see. It'll
              make us all feel better. You
              can't be unhappy and be at the
              seaside. It's just impossible.
              It's what they call a law of
              physics.

156A   I/E. MORRIS OXFORD - SEASIDE PROMENADE - DAY   156A

         Dirty brown Atlantic rollers lollop onto a stony beach.
         Ratty looking seagulls do somersaults. Sylvia stares at
         it. Her face full of defeat. She turns. In the car,
         Frieda's nose is pressed to the glass.

157   I/E. MORRIS OXFORD - DEVON ROAD - DAY - MOVING   157

         Sylvia drives down a twisting, single-lane Devon road
         with high banks on either side.

         She is going too fast.

         The Morris lurches around corners. In the back, Frieda
         begins to CRY.
                                              (CONTINUED)

157   CONTINUED: 157

Sylvia accelerates. Grim determination. And now as she
rounds a corner she sees fifty yards in front of her a
DELIVERY VAN, lumbering along the land.

Sylvia's FOOT hits the brake, and the car SKIDS, sliding
out of control towards the tractor, just missing, finally
coming to a halt angled awkwardly across the road.

Behind her, the van disappears around a corner, as if
nothing had happened.

Sylvia's head is on the steering wheel. Behind her,
Frieda and Nick scream in terror. Sylvia lifts her head,
as if realising what she almost did.

She turns to the children, tears in her eyes.

                    SYLVIA
          It's all right. It's all right.
          Don't you know? I'd never do
          anything to hurt you.

158   INT. COURT GREEN - UPSTAIRS - NIGHT   158

Rain LASHES against the windows. In their rooms, the
children sleep. Sylvia lies awake. Can't sleep.

Her BEDSIDE CLOCK says ten to four.

Outside, the WIND stirs in the trees. Through the window,
the branches of the great Wych-elm move like hands.

Sylvia stands at the window, looks out at the great tree
and the moon. Her face reflected.

HAMMERING of a typewriter --

159   INT. COURT GREEN - CONSERVATORY - NIGHT   159

-- as Sylvia writes with a feverish intensity, a fluidity
that is quite astonishing.

The poem seems to be falling full-formed onto the page,
as if she were not a writer but a medium, as if a
wormhole had opened up to another world and the fabric of
reality was tearing apart, letting whatever lies on the
other side of the mirror gush into reality.

Her face, rapt, as if she were transfigured by the act.

159A   EXT. COURT GREEN - CONSERVATORY - DAWN   159A

The night dissolves into a blue dawn. In the house, a
light at the window, and the CLATTERING of the typewriter
keys, and now:

                    SYLVIA (O.S.)
                    (furious)
            [Sylvia quotes from her poem
            "Daddy," lines 51-56]

165   INT. AL ALVAREZ' FLAT - NIGHT   165

Al sits in an armchair, watching Sylvia STAMP about as
she reads from a sheaf of papers. He looks like someone
trying to ride out a hurricane lashed a telegraph pole.

                    SYLVIA (CONT'D)
            [Sylvia quotes from her poem
            "Daddy," lines 71-80]

Alvarez, speechless.

                    ALVAREZ
            It's...

                    SYLVIA
            It's what? What is it?

                    ALVAREZ
            It's... it's just... I'm sorry,
            forgive me, I don't know what to
            say.

                    SYLVIA
            Is it any good?

                    ALVAREZ
            Good God, yes.

166   EXT. HAMPSTEAD - NIGHT   166

Alvarez walks Sylvia to the car.

                    ALVAREZ
            That one about the girl... the
            one with the Electra complex and
            the Nazi father... who she
            marries and then murders.
                    (MORE)

                                            (CONTINUED)

166   CONTINUED: 166

                    ALVAREZ (cont'd)
              What a horrifying little
              fairytale <u>that</u> is.

Sylvia, not quite sure how to respond. Then:

                    SYLVIA
              I'm thinking of moving back to
              London. Soon as I'm settled, I'll
              bring you more.

They stop by the car. An awkward moment.

                    ALVAREZ
              Are you okay. Really?

                    SYLVIA
              Wonderful. Wonderful.

                    ALVAREZ
              It must have been very difficult.

                    SYLVIA
              Not at all. I didn't mind a bit.
              Ted's getting on with his life.
              I'm getting on with mine. Really,
              I've never been happier. And I've
              never written so much. It's as
              if, now he's gone, I can finally
              write. I wake up at three or
              four... that's the worst time...
              and write till dawn.
                    (beat)
              I really feel like God is talking
              through me.

Alvarez, with no idea how to respond.

CAROLS play on a radio as --

167   EXT. FITZROY SQUARE - NIGHT - WINTER   167

-- SNOW falls in a London square, starting to settle now,
an inch deep. Light burns in an upstairs window by a BLUE
PLAQUE that says "D H LAWRENCE LIVED HERE".

SUPER: LONDON, DECEMBER 1961

168   INT. FITZROY SQUARE - NIGHT   168

Frieda helps Sylvia, who's singing along with the radio,
place HOME-MADE DECORATIONS on a four-foot high FAKE
CHRISTMAS tree, watched in dumb amazement by Nick, who's
propped up on the sofa.

                                        (CONTINUED)

168   CONTINUED: 168

The flat is now unfurnished, and painted white. It feels
stark, like the inside of a refrigerator. There is a kind
of beauty to it, but you can't help noticing that there
are no curtains at the windows (and there never will be).
On the mantelpiece is a conspicuous home-made POOR BOX.

Sylvia tops off the Christmas tree with an angel made out
of the inside of a toilet roll, a paper plate, and a ping
pong ball, then stands back to admire her work.

                    SYLVIA
          There! What do you think?

The LIGHTS go out.

170   INT. PROFESSOR THOMAS' FLAT - HALLWAY - NIGHT   170

BLACKNESS. SOUND of FRANTIC KNOCKING.

                    SYLVIA (O.S.)
                 (behind a door)
          Help! Please! Help!

                    PROFESSOR THOMAS (O.S.)
                 (very testy)
          All right, all right.

Now the black glimmers into candlelit gloom as a MIDDLE
AGED MAN (PROFESSOR THOMAS), candle in hand, approaches
the door. The Professor is middle aged, with an academic,
pedantic air, but his knit cardigan is missing a button
and his slippers have seen better days. He opens the
door, to reveal a distraught Sylvia.

                    SYLVIA
                 (seeing his candle)
          Oh, my God, it's happened to you
          as well!

                    PROFESSOR THOMAS
          What? What? You'll have to speak
          up.

He fiddles with his HEARING AID, which WHISTLES.

                    SYLVIA
          I've just moved in upstairs. But
          there's no light. There's no
          heat. We can't cook. There's no
          hot water. My babies are freezing
          to death...

                                                      (CONTINUED)

170   CONTINUED: 170

                    PROFESSOR THOMAS
          It's a power cut.
                    (off her blank look)
          Just at the moment when we most
          need heat and light to sustain
          life itself, the government shuts
          the electricity off.

                    SYLVIA
          Why?

                    PROFESSOR THOMAS
          To build the national character.

Sylvia, with no idea if he is joking or not.

171   INT. FITZROY SQUARE - KITCHEN - NIGHT   171

WHOOMPH! A gas ring ignites. Professor Thomas uses it to
light candles, which he's brought with him.

                    PROFESSOR THOMAS
          Keep the stove on for heat, and
          to boil water for washing. Here
          are some spare candles and
          matches...

                    SYLVIA
          Thank you so much. You must think
          I'm a stupid American bitch.

                    PROFESSOR THOMAS
          Not at all, my dear. I assumed
          you were Canadian.

Sylvia snorts with laughter, realizing she has found a
real ally in this funny old man.

                    SYLVIA
          It's been so hard, that's all.
          Being all alone. I wasn't made to
          be alone.

                    PROFESSOR THOMAS
          None of us is.

173   I/E. FITZROY SQUARE - DAY   173

Snow lies two feet deep, and it's STILL snowing. Wind
whips the flakes into chill flurries. It is as if London
has been transplanted to deepest Siberia.

                                        (CONTINUED)

173   CONTINUED: 173

KNOCKING ON A DOOR. Sylvia opens it, to Ted. He has a
bag, and is covered in snow.

Sylvia still looks thin, and tired, and from her SNIFFLES
she obviously can't shake the flu.

                    TED
          I brought some presents. For the
          children.

Reluctantly, Sylvia lets him in.

173A   INT. FITZROY SQUARE - DAY   173A

Ted stamps snow from his feet.

                    SYLVIA
          Nick's through there. Frieda, go
          and play with Daddy.

Frieda hangs on to her legs, afraid. Ted dumps the bag on
the floor, stands there awkwardly. Frieda, seeing a
PRESENT sticking out, runs over and grabs it then takes
it through to the lounge to open it. Ted hands a RUBBER
DUCK to Nick, who stares at it blankly.

                    TED
          I didn't just come to see them.
               (off her silence)
          For God's sake, it's Christmas. I
          wanted to see how you were doing.
          I mean, if you were all right...

He tails off. Each of them searches the other's eyes.

                    TED (CONT'D)
          Can't we forget about what's
          happened... just for an hour?
          Talk to each other like
          reasonable people?

                    SYLVIA
          All right. Sit down. We'll talk.

Ted, a little nervous, takes off his coat and scarf and
sits on a kitchen chair. Sylvia sits across the kitchen
table. An awkward silence, the CAROLS suddenly loud.

                    SYLVIA (CONT'D)
          So, are you still fucking her?

173AA   EXT. FITZROY SQUARE - DAY   173AA

Ted stalks away, hunched against the sleet.

Up at the first-floor window, behind him, Sylvia watches him go. She puts a palm against the glass.

He never looks back.

175   INT. AL ALVAREZ' FLAT - NIGHT   175

Alvarez is leafing through a SHEAF OF POEMS Sylvia has brought him.

She's wearing her hair down again, and has on clothes which are uncharacteristically vampish. She's also wearing make-up. She has an intense, rapt air, like 'the priestess emptied out by the rites of her cult'.

> ALVAREZ
> (leafing though poems)
> This one is stunning. And this one -- LADY LAZARUS --about the failed suicides. The despair... the overpowering sense of foreboding... and yet no hysteria or anger, or any appeal for sympathy. Such a wealth of imagery... and such horrors... but expressed with such coolness... like a murderer's confession...

He tails off, realising that Sylvia isn't listening.

> ALVAREZ
> The novel... have you got a title yet?

> SYLVIA
> (bored)
> The Bell Jar.

> ALVAREZ
> And when's it out?

> SYLVIA
> (shrugs)
> The New Year.

> ALVAREZ
> I can't wait.

(CONTINUED)

                              SYLVIA
                    It's a pot-boiler.

Said with real steel, a final judgement. Alvarez, running
out of things to say.

                              SYLVIA
                    Do you think you could get me an
                    ashtray?

A beat. Alvarez gets up to find one. Sylvia lights a
cigarette. He returns.

                              ALVAREZ
                    I didn't know you smoked.

                              SYLVIA
                    I don't. What I mean is, I've
                    started. I'm trying some new
                    things.

                              ALVAREZ
                    Really? Like what?

                              SYLVIA
                         (big drag)
                    I'm thinking of taking a lover.

                              ALVAREZ
                    How glamorous! Who is he?

Sylvia looks right into his eyes. Alvarez is so stunned
he doesn't know what to do. Sylvia, fighting her
emotions.

                              ALVAREZ (CONT'D)
                    I know what you're going through.

                              SYLVIA
                    No, you don't. Nobody does.

                              ALVAREZ
                    I do. I'm like you. One of the
                    undead.

Sylvia, instantly understanding.

                              SYLVIA
                         (a hunger to talk about
                          this)
                    How?

>   ALVAREZ
>   The same as you. Sleeping pills.
>   Only I took too many. Everybody
>   does, don't they?

Sylvia inspects his face with new eyes. Her lip works as
a great gush of emotion wells up inside her.

>   SYLVIA
>   Sometimes I think I'm not solid
>   at all. It's as if I'm hollow.
>   With nothing behind the eyes. A
>   negative of a person. As if I
>   never thought anything, wrote
>   anything, felt anything. And all
>   I want to do is crawl back into
>   the womb.

>   ALVAREZ
>   One thing I know about death. It
>   isn't a homecoming. Or a release.
>   Or a spiritual experience, or a
>   consummation devoutly to be
>   wish'd. It isn't anything. It's
>   just a great big bugger all.

Sylvia, desperately fighting tears through all of this.
She wipes away a rogue drop.

>   SYLVIA
>   But what do you do when things
>   have gone as wrong as they can,
>   and they keep getting worse, and
>   worse, and worse?

>   ALVAREZ
>   Keep going.

Sylvia grips his hand tight.

>   ALVAREZ
>   Listen... you're beautiful.
>   You've a wonderful mind. You're a
>   great poet. But you and Ted...
>   you understood each other in ways
>   most people can only dream about.
>   For God's sake don't throw it all
>   away just because of...

>   SYLVIA
>   (interrupting)
>   I don't want to hear her name!

175   CONTINUED: (3)   175

                         ALVAREZ
                    ...an affair.

176   INT. BOOKSHOP - DAY   176

        Sylvia browses the shelves looking for something very
        specific. She finds it: A BIG RED VOLUME of Shakespeare,
        exactly like the one of Ted's she destroyed.

178   I/E. TED'S FLAT - DAY   178

        Sylvia stands in front of a door, nervous. She is dressed
        as we are used to seeing her, smart, classic lines, very
        American. She has a HEAVY BAG.

        She composes herself, straightens something, KNOCKS.

        The door opens. It's Ted.

                         SYLVIA
                    I don't want to be your enemy.

        Sylvia peers past him, as if to check for Assia.

                         TED
                    She isn't here.

        He opens the door to let her in. Sylvia enters, following
        Ted. The place is in complete chaos. A typewriter at a
        desk, half buried under a heap of papers. Books and
        clothes strewn over the floor. An index to his mental
        state. Nothing to suggest Assia.

        What there is, however, on Ted's cluttered desk, is a RED
        VOLUME OF SHAKESPEARE, as if the one Sylvia destroyed had
        been somehow reincarnated.

                         TED
                    Al can't say enough about your
                    new stuff. He's like a teenager.
                    But he means it. And he's
                    nobody's fool.

        But Sylvia's not listening because she can't take her
        eyes off the Shakespeare. Ted can't figure her out.

        An awkward silence.

                         TED (CONT'D)
                    Do you want a cup of tea or
                    something?

                                                    (CONTINUED)

178   CONTINUED: 178

                          SYLVIA
                       (seizing her
                        opportunity)
                 Yes, yes please.

Ted heads into the kitchen. Sylvia immediately heads over
to the desk, opens the Shakespeare.

"TO TED, WITH ALL MY LOVE, ASSIA".

In the kitchen, Ted pulls a bottle of milk out of the
fridge, smells it. It's off. He goes to the door.

                          TED
                 Do you mind powdered?

But the room is empty. His confusion.

181   EXT. LONDON STREET - NIGHT   181

           With Sylvia as she walks away through the snow.

182   INT. PROFESSOR THOMAS' FLAT - BEDROOM - NIGHT   182

           Professor Thomas turns in bed, unable to sleep on account
           of the MUSIC that is coming down through the floorboards
           from the upstairs flat.

           He checks the clock: 3.30 am.

           He pulls the pillow over his head, but it doesn't help.

           Abruptly, the music stops.

           The professor cautiously pulls his head out from under
           the pillow. Is it going to start up again? No. He sighs,
           stretches out, plumps up the pillow, luxuriates into it.

           Sleep, blessed sleep.

           A KNOCK on the door.

           Professor Thomas lets out a cry of frustration.

183   INT. PROFESSOR THOMAS' FLAT - HALLWAY - NIGHT   183

           The professor yanks open the door. Sylvia stands there,
           fully dressed. She looks ghastly. Great tears are
           coursing down her cheeks. She seems truly desperate.

                                                        (CONTINUED)

                         SYLVIA
              I'm going to die soon... and who
              will look after my babies?

184   INT. PROFESSOR THOMAS' FLAT - LIVING ROOM - DAY   184

The living room is untidy, strewn with papers and books
about art. Professor Thomas clears a shabby sofa.

                         PROFESSOR THOMAS
              My dear... sit down, please.

                         SYLVIA
              I don't want to die. There's so
              much I still have to do...

                         PROFESSOR THOMAS
              But, Mrs Hughes, why on earth do
              you think you're going to die?
              You're a strong, healthy woman.
              It's just a touch of flu, that's
              all. I dare say you're a little
              delirious from the fever.

                         SYLVIA
              No, no, you don't understand...
              I'm not ill.

                         PROFESSOR THOMAS
              Even so, perhaps I should call a
              doctor.

Sylvia jumps, as if in terror.

                         SYLVIA
              No! No doctors! Don't you know
              what they do to you? Wire you up
              to the eastern grid and fill you
              full of sparks!

                         PROFESSOR THOMAS
                    (taken aback)
              Please... please, my dear... I
              didn't mean to...

                         SYLVIA
              I'm sorry... it's just that I'm
              so terribly on edge.
                    (through tears)
              It's all my fault. All I could
              think about what would happen if
              someone took him away from me.
                    (MORE)

                                           (CONTINUED)

184   CONTINUED: 184
                              SYLVIA (cont'd)
                    If you fear a thing enough that
                    can make it happen, don't you
                    see? That woman - I conjured her
                    up. I invented her. Do you
                    understand?

                         PROFESSOR THOMAS
                    Perhaps a little.

Professor Thomas offers her a big cotton handkerchief.

                              SYLVIA
                    The nights are the worst. I can't
                    sleep. If only I could sleep a
                    little, just a little... and then
                    I'm exhausted all day...

                         PROFESSOR THOMAS
                    Perhaps you could get someone to
                    help with the children.

                              SYLVIA
                         (suddenly rising)
                    Oh, God! I left them all alone!

                         PROFESSOR THOMAS
                    I'm sure they're fine. But
                    perhaps if you're feeling a
                    little better you might go and
                    see if they are all right.

                              SYLVIA
                         (drying her eyes)
                    Yes, yes. Thank you so much.
                         (touching his arm)
                    You remind me a little of my
                    father.

Professor Thomas smiles.

186   INT. FITZROY SQUARE - BEDROOM - DAY   186

Frieda plays on the floor. Sylvia sits at her desk,
opening BILLS. Electricity, gas, rent. They are red. A
beat as she reads each one, then CRUMPLES it up and drops
it into a waste basket.

Straws, piling up on a camel's back.

Frieda toddles over.

                              FRIEDA
                    Mummy, I'm hun-gry.

                                              (CONTINUED)

Now a KNOCK at the door makes her jump.

She opens the door. It's Professor Thomas.

>   SYLVIA
>   Yes?

She's brittle, secretarial almost.

>   PROFESSOR THOMAS
>   I just came to make sure you were
>   all right.

>   SYLVIA
>   (sharply)
>   Why shouldn't I be?

>   PROFESSOR THOMAS
>   The other night...

>   SYLVIA
>   (very cool)
>   Oh, that. I'm sorry I was so
>   silly. Do me a favour, won't you,
>   and forget about it.

>   PROFESSOR THOMAS
>   (deeply embarrassed)
>   Yes... yes... of course.

Behind Sylvia, Frieda appears again.

>   SYLVIA
>   Now if you'll excuse me, I have
>   to get the children their lunch.

>   PROFESSOR THOMAS
>   I'm very sorry to have troubled
>   you.

Sylvia closes the door, heads towards the kitchen.

>   SYLVIA
>   (to Frieda)
>   Now, what would you like? There's
>   beans, or spaghetti hoops, or I
>   could make cheese on toast, or we
>   could have muffins...

She opens the kitchen cupboard.

It is completely empty, totally bare. Sylvia's shock.

(CONTINUED)

186   CONTINUED: (2)   186

                              SYLVIA
                    Or... what about...

She pulls open the fridge.

It too is empty. Just a bottle of milk with an inch
remaining and a plate of hard butter.

Sylvia puts her hand to her head, as if dizzy.

Frieda, picking up on her panic.

                              FRIEDA
                    I'm hun-gry.

187   I/E. PHONE BOX - FITZROY SQUARE - DAY   187

SYLVIA'S HANDS, dialling a number. Now we see she's,
coatless and freezing, ADDRESS BOOK in hand, with Frieda
in the phone box, Nick's pram outside.

No answer. She tries another.

It RINGS and RINGS. Now someone answers. The PIPS go.

                              SYLVIA
                         (not used to
                          phoneboxes)
                    Hello? Hello?
                         (the PIPS)
                    Hello?
                         (pushes the coin in the
                          hole)
                    Kate! Kate, it's Sylvia... I... I
                    just... I just wondered if I
                    could come round to see you...

                         FIRST WOMAN (V.O.)
                         (on phone)
                    Oh, Sylvia. It would be lovely to
                    see you, but...

                                        JUMP CUT TO:

189   SAME - ANOTHER CALL   189

Sylvia, taking the hit from:

189   CONTINUED: 189

                    SECOND WOMAN (V.O.)
                        (on phone)
              ... Robin and I are going down to
              the country this weekend...

                                              JUMP CUT TO:

190   SAME - ANOTHER CALL   190

                    THIRD WOMAN (V.O.)
                        (on phone)
              What about next week sometime?

Sylvia's face, a mask of defeat. She hangs up without
answering, unable to think what to do. An OLD MAN raps on
the window, points at his watch. Sylvia goes back into
her address book, finds a number, dials it.

It RINGS, picks up. The PIPS. She stuffs in a penny.

A MAN'S VOICE answers.

                    SYLVIA
                    (only just holding it
                     together)
              Please... Dr Hawkins, please... I
              can't do it any more. It's too
              much. Oh, God, help me, please.

The MAN'S VOICE talks. We can't hear what he's saying,
but he sounds calm, reassuring. Fatherlike.

Sylvia, listening to his instructions.

190A   EXT. FITZROY SQUARE - NIGHT   190A

The street, arctic. A light burns in Sylvia's window.

191   INT. FITZROY SQUARE - BEDROOM - NIGHT   191

Sylvia, in her nightdress, ready for bed. The clock says
ten thirty.

TWO BOTTLES OF PILLS sit on a bedside table, with a GLASS
OF WATER.

Sylvia takes one of the bottles, unscrews the lid. She
tips out a handful of pills, stares at them. For a moment
we think she's going to take them all. But she tips back
all but two.

                                              (CONTINUED)

191   CONTINUED: 191

She takes the pills and washes them down with water, then
sits on the edge of the bed. She seems numb, almost
blank, perhaps dreading the night ahead.

Now she turns the light off and gets into bed.

Her, eyes, open.

195   INT. FITZROY SQUARE - BEDROOM - NIGHT   195

The clock says four. An eerie noise, almost like an
animal in distress.

It's Sylvia, awake, crying.

The clock. The seconds tick past, one by one.

195A   INT. FITZROY SQUARE - BEDROOM - DAWN   195A

Blue light. The clock says six.

Sylvia, still awake.

She pulls herself vertical. She hasn't slept.

She takes the second of the two pill bottles, pours out a
couple of pills, takes them with the glass of water.

A beat. The day stretches ahead of her, blank.

She tries to pull herself together.

196   INT. FITZROY SQUARE - KITCHEN - DAY   196

BAGS OF SHOPPING on the kitchen table. Sylvia is cooking
a late breakfast of eggs, bacon, sausage. Frieda and Nick
watch as Sylvia talks to them, energetic and bright.

                    SYLVIA
          I feel like I haven't eaten for a
          hundred years, don't you?
                    (to Frieda)
          Do you want more toast, darling?
          You haven't eaten nearly enough.

196A   INT. FITZROY SQUARE - DOWNSTAIRS HALLWAY - DAY 196A

Sylvia is mandhandling a PRAM containing Nick through the
hallway, with Frieda in tow. At that moment the door
opens to admit Professor Thomas.

                                          (CONTINUED)

196A   CONTINUED:

He takes off his hat to her, rather formally, continuing
the tone of their last meeting.

                    PROFESSOR THOMAS
               Mrs Hughes...

                    SYLVIA
               Oh, Professor Thomas! How lovely
               to see you. The other day... I'm
               sorry I was so rude. You were
               right. I talked to the doctor,
               and he gave me some pills, and
               now I feel much better, and he's
               sending a nurse round to help me
               out with the children. And I'm
               eating properly again, and I've
               got a routine...

                    PROFESSOR THOMAS
               Are you sleeping any better?

                    SYLVIA
               No, no, but I'm sure I will. And
               now there's just one more thing I
               have to do and then everything's
               going to be all right. Do you
               mind?

Professor Thomas squeezes up against the wall as she
wrangles the pram past him and out into the snow covered
square. She seems like a woman on a mission.

                    PROFESSOR THOMAS
               Good day, Mrs Hughes.

He watches her go, then shuts the door.

198A   EXT. FITZROY SQUARE - DAY   198A

Sylvia crosses the freezing square, pushing the pram and
pulling Frieda along, towards the telephone box.

198B   I/E. FITZROY SQUARE - PHONE BOX - DAY   198B

Sylvia's fingers hover over the dial. It's as if she's
afraid to dial, but has no choice. Her tension. Now she
dials. The phone RINGS and RINGS. Now someone picks up.

                                             (CONTINUED)

198B   CONTINUED:

>   TED (V.O.)
>   Hello?

204   INT. FITZROY SQUARE - BEDROOM - NIGHT   204

Sylvia sits in front of the dressing table mirror in a
slip. A METALLIC COCKTAIL DRESS hangs on the wardrobe
door behind her. Her hair is in curlers.

She applies make up, very carefully.

She paints her mouth crimson, just as we saw her at the
beginning.

Now she pulls out the curlers. Her hair falls down. She
shakes it out.

She looks at her watch. It's time.

A KNOCK at the door.

207   EXT. FITZROY SQUARE - HALLWAY/DOOR - NIGHT   207

Sylvia opens the door. It's Ted. He takes in the effect.
With the hair and lipstick, she looks strikingly like she
did the first time he ever set eyes on her.

>   TED
>   You look... very nice.

>   SYLVIA
>   Do I?

They both stand there a moment, a little embarrassed,
almost like teenagers on a first date.

>   SYLVIA
>   You'd better come in.

208   INT. FITZROY SQUARE - LIVING ROOM - NIGHT   208

Ted, pulling off his coat and scarf.

>   SYLVIA
>   (proffering wine)
>   Drink?

>   TED
>   Thanks. Look...

She takes his coat and scarf. Totally calm, in control.
>   (CONTINUED)

208 CONTINUED: 208

> TED
> ...you might as well know. People
> say you've been acting strange
> for weeks. Alvarez told me you
> made a pass at him. Someone else
> said you're on pills. What's this
> all about?

> SYLVIA
> What it's always been about.

Without warning, she KISSES him, hard, on the mouth.
Initially Ted is taken aback... he stiffens, resists, but
then he relaxes into it. Gradually he starts to hold her
like a lover, the tenderness flowing back like a stream,
then a river, then a flood.

He kisses her on the neck. His cheek. Sylvia opens her
mouth to bite it, remembering. But this time kisses it.

209   INT. FITZROY SQUARE - BEDROOM - NIGHT   209

Ted lowers Sylvia onto the bed. And it begins, the sex of
people who have been starved of each other for whole
lifetimes, whose hunger for each other is bottomless. But
it also has a tenderness to it, a real gentleness we have
hardly seen before.

By the end of it both of them are crying.

210   INT. FITZROY SQUARE - BEDROOM - NIGHT - LATER   210

They lie together, spoons.

> TED
> God, I've missed you.

> SYLVIA
> I almost went mad.
>   (beat)
> We're not two people. We never
> were. Even before we met, we were
> just half people. With these big
> ripping gaping holes in us shaped
> like the other person. And
> then... we found each other...
> and we were finally the whole
> person. But then we couldn't
> stand it, it was as if we
> couldn't stand being happy, so we
> tore ourself in half again.
>   (MORE)

210   CONTINUED: 210

                          SYLVIA (cont'd)
                Each of us, without the other,
                just half a person. Bleeding for
                lack of love.
                          (turning to him)
                The children, they've missed you
                so much. They need a father, Ted.
                We've still got that beautiful
                house, remember? In the spring,
                we'll move back to Devon.

Ted's face, wanting to believe this can happen.

                          SYLVIA (CONT'D)
                We'll go back to Devon and all
                we'll have is ourselves and the
                children and our work. Everything
                that's happened, the summer and
                the fall and this goddamn winter,
                it'll all fade away and by the
                time the leaves are out it'll
                just seem like some terrible
                nightmare that we finally woke
                out of. It'll be as if nothing
                every happened. And there'll be
                nothing left in the whole world
                to say that it did.

As she speaks, Ted's face seems to fill with a terrible
knowledge. His expression becomes full of grief.

                          SYLVIA
                You don't love her like you love
                me. What you have with her...it's
                not the same. You know it isn't.
                Is it?
                          (off his silence)
                You'll never have with her what
                you have with me.

                          TED
                I know.

                          SYLVIA
                So why can't you leave her?

                          TED
                She's pregnant.

211   EXT. FITZROY SQUARE - NIGHT   211

Ted walks away from the house.

212   INT. FITZROY SQUARE - BEDROOM - NIGHT   212

Sylvia sits on the rumpled bed with her back to us,
completely naked. Completely still.

217   EXT. FITZROY SQUARE - NIGHT   217

The street is dark. A LIGHT burns in Sylvia's window. Her
silhouette. Now she disappears.

A KNOCK at a door

218   INT. PROFESSOR THOMAS' FLAT - HALLWAY - NIGHT   218

Professor Thomas opens the door. It's Sylvia. She seems
strangely bright. She has a purse with her.

                    PROFESSOR THOMAS
          Mrs. Hughes. Is something wrong?

                    SYLVIA
          Oh, no, no. Not really. It's
          just, isn't it silly? I forgot to
          buy stamps. And I need them,
          because it's airmail for America,
          and they have to go in the box
          tonight.

                    PROFESSOR THOMAS
          Can't you post them tomorrow?

                    SYLVIA
          No, no, they have to go in
          tonight, because there's a nurse
          coming in the morning.

Professor Thomas, unable to see the logic of this.

                    SYLVIA
          I'm so sorry to bother you. I
          won't do it again, I promise.

The Professor sighs, disappears, and returns with stamps.
Sylvia fishes in her purse.

                    PROFESSOR THOMAS
          Please.

                                              (CONTINUED)

218   CONTINUED: 218

>   SYLVIA
>   Oh, but I must pay you. Or I
>   won't be right with my conscience
>   before God, will I? Will five
>   shillings do?

She holds out the money.

>   PROFESSOR THOMAS
>   Thank you. And... good night.

He closes the door and heads into the bathroom, where he
runs a glass of water. As he emerges to go to bed,
however, he notices a THIN RIBBON OF LIGHT under his
door. He opens the door to see --

219   INT. FITZROY SQUARE - SHARED HALLWAY - NIGHT   219

-- Sylvia, motionless in the corridor, rapt, fixated by
something above eye level. There's nothing there but a
flyblown light fitting.

>   PROFESSOR THOMAS
>   Mrs. Hughes.

Sylvia looks towards him, eyes shining.

>   PROFESSOR THOMAS (CONT'D)
>   Perhaps you'd like me to call
>   someone.

>   SYLVIA
>   Oh, no! Please don't do that. I'm
>   having the most marvellous dream.
>   A most wonderful vision!

She goes back to her hallucination. Her face, seraphic,
bathed in light, radiant, sparkling.

Professor Thomas closes the door. The ribbon of light.
Guilt nags at his brain. He opens the door again.

>   PROFESSOR THOMAS
>   I really think...

But she's gone.

220   INT. PROFESSOR THOMAS' FLAT - BEDROOM - NIGHT   220

Professor Thomas gets into bed, flops onto the pillow.

                                                   (CONTINUED)

220   CONTINUED:

Now, from the flat above, he becomes aware of MUSIC. It's
Beethoven, one of the late quartets that has been our
theme. Slow, majestic, tragic, unbearably moving.

Accompanying it, the sound of FOOTSTEPS on a wooden
floor.

Professor Thomas reaches to remove his HEARING AID. But
as he does the music suddenly STOPS.

Now the MUSIC starts up again.

Professor Thomas GROANS, and removes his hearing aid.

223   INT. FITZROY SQUARE - KITCHEN - NIGHT   223

The MUSIC plays, unbearably moving.

Sylvia is buttering bread. She puts it on plates, fills
two GLASSES with MILK, and puts the whole lot on a TRAY.

Visible on the kitchen table are a roll of tape,
SCISSORS, and a pile of BATH towels.

224   INT. FITZROY SQUARE - CHILDREN'S BEDROOM - NIGHT   224

Sylvia enters with the tray of bread and milk. She
carefully places it on the bedside table.

Now she opens the bedroom window. Her breath freezes
instantly in the air. The cold seems to stop her in her
tracks for a moment. She looks over to the children, and
finds a couple of EXTRA BLANKETS which she gently places
over them, careful not to wake them.

225A   INT. FITZROY SQUARE - NIGHT   225A

Sylvia goes to the front door, locks it.

She goes into the kitchen, takes a TEA TOWEL from the bar
on the oven door.

So far it has all been done methodically, but it is as if
the tea towel suddenly brings her up with the reality of
what she is about to do.

Just for a moment, it looks as though her face might
crumple, but then she masters herself.

She closes the kitchen door, shutting us out.

                                                    (CONTINUED)

225A   CONTINUED: 225A

        CLOSING IN on the door as the music CRESCENDOS, and then
        on the final climactic chord, we CUT TO:

226   BLACK   226

        SOUND of a gramophone needle CLICKING in its groove.

226A   EXT. FITZROY SQUARE - MORNING   226A

        The morning is crystal clear, the perfect blue sky the
        sign of a hard frost. Sound carries like a hammer on an
        anvil.

        We're MOVING with a YOUNG WOMAN (Myra Norris) in a
        Nurse's blue coat, as she crosses the square to the front
        door of Sylvia and the Professor's flats.

        She RINGS the doorbell marked 'HUGHES'. Nothing. She
        rings again. Still nothing.

        A CHILD'S CRYING makes her look up.

        It's Frieda, at the open window, freezing and distressed.

        Myra, suddenly frightened.

        She RUNS across the square to the phone box where a
        MIDDLE AGED MAN (CHARLES LANGRIDGE) is making a phone
        call, pulls him out.

                        MYRA NORRIS
                        (to Langridge)
                Please, would you help me? I
                think something terrible may have
                happened.

228   BLACK   228

        A BUMP. And then a CRASH. And then a BIGGER CRASH as --

229   INT. FITZROY SQUARE - DAY   229

        -- a MIDDLE AGED MAN (CHARLES LANGRIDGE) in builder's
        clothes KICKS down the door and LURCHES into the room,
        we've been inside. A YOUNG WOMAN in a nurse's uniform
        (MYRA NORRIS) follows him, tentatively. Langridge looks
        around, COUGHS.

                                                        (CONTINUED)

229   CONTINUED: 229

He throws the windows open as Myra follows the crying to
the children's bedroom door. She PULLS away the bath
towels and the tapes and --

230   INT. FITZROY SQUARE - CHILDREN'S BEDROOM - DAY   230

-- SCOOPS UP the freezing children from their beds.

231   INT. FITZROY SQUARE - LIVING ROOM - DAY   231

Langridge tries the kitchen door. It won't budge.
Something's blocking it from the inside.

He SHOULDERS the door, and it opens a crack. MORE TOWELS
have been stuffed under the door, blocking it from
opening. He kicks them away, and the door opens.

The gas almost chokes him. When he finally stops coughing
and looks inside, his face goes ashen.

232   EXT. FITZROY SQUARE - DAY - LATER   232

An AMBULANCE is parked outside the house.

TWO AMBULANCEMEN emerge from the house, using a stretcher
to remove a BODY under a RED BLANKET.

They shunt the stretcher into the vehicle.

On the SLAM of the doors, cut to:

233   INT. FITZROY SQUARE - KITCHEN - DAY   233

A FAT POLICEMAN leans into CAMERA. He gently removes a
FOLDED TEA TOWEL from the floor of the oven. It still
bears the imprint of a human head.

                         POLICEMAN
                  The funny thing is...

He extricates himself from the oven, holding the tea-
towel very carefully, as if it were evidence.

                    POLICEMAN (CONT'D)
               ...they generally leave a note.

He looks through the door to --

234   INT. FITZROY SQUARE - LIVING ROOM - CONTINUOUS   234

-- Ted, standing by Sylvia's desk, in front of the
window, dumb with grief. The windows are still open.

The desk is perfectly neat. Typewriter, a jam jar with
pens, Roget's thesaurus, a pile of typing paper, and in
the centre of it all a BOUND MANUSCRIPT. Ted has it open,
is staring at words on a page. The title: 'EDGE'.

                    TED
          What did you say?

                    POLICEMAN
          They usually leave a note.

                    TED
          She did.

Now we see the title of the book:

                    ~~DADDY~~
                    ARIEL
          BY SYLVIA PLATH

Ted opens it. A poem called EDGE. It fills the screen.

(NOTE: FOR LEGAL REASONS ONLY THE LINES QUOTED BELOW MAY
BE SHOWN)

                    SYLVIA (V.O.)
          The woman is perfected.

235   INT. ST PANCRAS MORTUARY - DAY   235

Ted lifts a WHITE SHROUD to reveal Sylvia's body, her
hair down, Ophelia-like.

MOVING slowly around the two of them as Ted says his
final goodbye, holding her hand.

                    SYLVIA (V.O.)
          [Sylvia quotes from her poem
          "Edge," lines 2-5]

Ted gently strokes Sylvia's hair. As we GLIDE AROUND, we
see that the white shroud does indeed seem like some kind
of toga. At the bottom, her naked feet.

                    SYLVIA (V.O.) (CONT'D)
          [Sylvia quotes from her poem
          "Edge," lines 6-8]

                                        (CONTINUED)

235   CONTINUED: 235

Ted leans down and kisses her on the forehead.

238   CARDS ON BLACK   238

Sylvia Plath's <u>Ariel</u> was published in 1965. An immediate success, it became one of the best-selling volumes of poetry of the twentieth century.

Al Alvarez, the foremost champion of her work, subsequently published a classic study of suicide, THE SAVAGE GOD, which revealed to the public for the first time the circumstances of her death.

Ted Hughes went on to become one of Britain's most celebrated literary figures, and was ultimately accorded Britain's highest poetic honour by being appointed Poet Laureate.

In 1998 he broke a forty-year silence about his life with Sylvia Plath with the unexpected publication of an acclaimed poetic memoir, BIRTHDAY LETTERS.

He died of cancer a few months later.

THE END

Sylvia Plath (Gwyneth Paltrow) and Ted Hughes (Daniel Craig) dancing, at their very first meeting.

Sylvia (Gwyneth Paltrow) racing down the streets of Cambridge, England, on her bicycle.

Sylvia (Gwyneth Paltrow) seeing Ted for the first time, at the magazine launch party at the Women's Union in Cambridge.

Ted (Daniel Craig) and Sylvia (Gwyneth Paltrow) on the river in Cambridge.

Ted (Daniel Craig) guiding the punt.

Sylvia (Gwyneth Paltrow) with Ted (Daniel Craig) at Ted's house in London.

Ted (Daniel Craig) and Sylvia (Gwyneth Paltrow) at the altar with the vicar (Derek Payne).

Sylvia (Gwyneth Paltrow) is greeted by her mother, Aurelia (Blythe Danner), with Ted (Daniel Craig) following behind, as they arrive at Aurelia's house in the United States.

Ted (Daniel Craig)

Aurelia Plath (Blythe Danner), Sylvia's mother

Sylvia (Gwyneth Paltrow) preparing food before the party with her mother (Blythe Danner).

Sylvia (Gwyneth Paltrow) enjoying the party with Ted (Daniel Craig).

Aurelia Plath (Blythe Danner) exchanging pleasantries with Ted (Daniel Craig) as Sylvia (Gwyneth Paltrow) looks on.

Sylvia (Gwyneth Paltrow) proudly watches her new husband with her mother (Blythe Danner).

Ted (Daniel Craig) and Sylvia (Gwyneth Paltrow) at their honeymoon vacation on Cape Cod.

Sylvia (Gwyneth Paltrow) and Ted (Daniel Craig) on vacation on Cape Cod.

Sylvia (Gwyneth Paltrow) experiencing writer's block on Cape Cod.

Sylvia (Gwyneth Paltrow) lecturing at Smith College.

Ted (Daniel Craig) delivering his lecture at Harvard.

The newly wed Sylvia (Gwyneth Paltrow) and Ted (Daniel Craig) enjoying themselves.

Sylvia (Gwyneth Paltrow) at the launch party in London for her first book *The Colossus*.

Sylvia (Gwyneth Paltrow) getting some inside information on the party attendees from Al Alvarez (Jared Harris).

Professor Thomas (Michael Gambon) trying to comfort Sylvia (Gwyneth Paltrow).

Sylvia (Gwyneth Paltrow) after she has separated from Ted.

Director Christine Jeffs with Daniel Craig

Director Christine Jeffs

Director Christine Jeffs with Director of Photography John Toon

THE GENESIS OF THE FILM

Four decades after her death, Sylvia Plath's unique voice continues to reach and inspire new readers. What they hear often changes their perceptions of themselves and those closest to them.

Among the many who count Sylvia as both influence and inspiration are the creative principals behind *Sylvia*: Academy Award-winning actress Gwyneth Paltrow, Academy Award-nominated producer Alison Owen, director Christine Jeffs, and screenwriter John Brownlow.

After years of envisioning the project, Owen commenced active development on Sylvia in early 1998 through her production company Ruby Films. She explains, "I've always been interested in Sylvia Plath; like lots of girls, I've been a fan since I was a teenager. I had always thought that Sylvia and Ted were a great love story. Ted published *Birthday Letters* just before his death; he'd been notoriously private in his life until then. But these last poems were wonderful works of art, very beautiful... and they opened up the subject of his relationship with Sylvia. It felt that there was somehow a tacit granting of permission to look at the subject.

"Sylvia did not really get acknowledged for her poetry until after her death, and this is the irony of the couple's story. She wanted two things out of her life: one was lasting acclaim and fame for her work and the other was the great love of a man. Ultimately, she was only able to get one by losing the other—which is her great tragedy."

Owen's first concern was to find a screenwriter who would treat the real-life subjects with respect and care. She had already been collaborating with John Brownlow on another project. The mere mention of Sylvia sparked Brownlow's interest instantly. He reflects, "It was Sylvia Plath's poetry that had led me to my decision, when at Oxford University, to switch from a mathematics degree to an English degree."

Brownlow originally comes from a documentary background, and as a result, comments Owen, "was meticulous in terms of the research. John employed a researcher who interviewed many of Sylvia and Ted's friends and acquaintances. Therefore, we had our own body of information in addition to all the source material that existed.

"He did an enormous amount of research, then he sat down and wrote, at which point he said that he felt the muse was sitting on his shoulder. The story unfolded in front of him, and I think that fluidity shows in John's screen-writing."

Brownlow confides, "I was initially cautious, not because of the potentially fraught nature of the project—I was formerly an investigative documentary filmmaker and therefore used to tackling controversial subjects—but because I did not know how I was going to put words into the mouths of two liter-ary giants. I also wanted to be sure that we were telling a story with universal appeal, rather than only speaking to poetry fans."

After his months of research, Brownlow "finally found the story that I had been looking for, which was to focus entirely on the relationship between Sylvia and Ted, more or less from the moment they met until the moment she died. It had to be romantic. This seemed to me to be the universal story, because here were two people who did what we all dream of—they met the person they were destined to be with. The problem was, they also had the capacity to destroy each other; you could even argue that that was what they found most attractive in each other. You don't have to have heard of Sylvia Plath and Ted Hughes to find theirs a compelling story, or to want to know how it will turn out."

In the summer of 2002, now well-nurtured by its producer and screen-writer, *Sylvia* still needed a director. Owen and Brownlow screened Christine Jeffs' debut feature *Rain*. The producer quickly sensed that Jeffs might be the one she was looking for: "More than anything we wanted a director who can move an audience, because that's ultimately what the film is going to succeed or fail on. When I saw *Rain*, I could not speak afterwards. It's an extraordinary film. We got in touch and, as it happened, Christine already knew a lot about Sylvia Plath and was a fan of hers."

Jeffs remembers, "I was on my farm in New Zealand and got a call from my agent, who said 'You've got to read this script.' When I realized that it was a movie about Sylvia Plath, it was a dream come true. The next step was to meet with Gwyneth and the financiers—one day I was on my farm with my horses and the next day I was flying to New York.

"*Sylvia* is very much a love story—and Sylvia's story, as she tries to be both a creative person and a mother. I was interested not only in the love story but also in the implications of two powerful creative forces being brought together and how that made their lives so difficult for each other."

In late October 2002, just weeks after Jeffs got the call at her farm, ten weeks of location filming started. The shoot took the filmmakers to London (at Shepperton Studios), Cambridge's Trinity College, Cornwall and, later, New Zealand (at Otago University; near Dunedin; on South Island). In and around these evocative locales, Gwyneth Paltrow and Daniel Craig became the long-awaited screen incarnations of an unforgettable couple as years of work came to full fruition.

THE CASTING

All actors have their dream roles, and Sylvia Plath has fascinated Gwyneth Paltrow for a decade. She notes, "In 1993, I was acting in the film *Mrs. Parker and the Vicious Circle*. Several of the women that I was working with told me that I should play Sylvia Plath one day. On the last day of shooting, they gifted me with a copy of *The Bell Jar*. I read it, and thought, 'She is fantastic.' I started reading more about Sylvia and more of her writing. So when Alison Owen approached me with this project a couple of years later, I was very interested!"

Owen had always had Paltrow in mind for the role of Sylvia, having produced one of the actress's notable early features, *Moonlight and Valentino*. Owen explains, "Once I decided to try and make the film, Gwyneth was the first person I called to ask about portraying Sylvia. She has enormous enthusiasm and passion for Sylvia, she looks like her, and she has the same kind of East Coast grace, ease, and intellectual strengths. Gwyneth always works well in period movies, since she has this beautiful quality about her that seems almost mercurial. She is a great actress with enormous emotional depth, and so she is able to fully take on a persona; it's almost like she inhabits Sylvia.

"One of the things that I'm most proud of with *Sylvia* is that you never feel like you're watching actors—you're caught up in the world and you feel like you're watching real people in that time."

Christine Jeffs concurs, saying that "once Gwyneth started to play Sylvia, it was very hard to separate Sylvia's character from Gwyneth. She *became* Sylvia to me, and it was strange to see her at the end of the day returned to looking like Gwyneth. She works instinctively and was passionate about playing the role, so her portrayal is very intuitive and emotional."

As expected, Paltrow researched her role extensively and spoke to a number of Sylvia's friends. The actress found that "people describe her as very alive and vivacious—but, at the same time, she was so complicated. She has never struck me as being a 'girl's girl'; she seems to have had difficult relationships with women."

It was Sylvia's relationship with Ted that most concerned the filmmakers, along with the portrayal of same. An actor who would have chemistry with Paltrow was sought. U.K. actor Daniel Craig had played a small but pivotal role in *Elizabeth* for producer Owen, and had since made his name on-screen in *Road to Perdition*. He had also maintained an interest in Ted Hughes for most of his life. He reports, "Since I was a child, I've had tapes of Ted Hughes reading his poetry.

"When I was at secondary school, we snuck in to see him when he spoke at the local grammar school."

Owen says, "We saw so many people for the role. It seemed that almost every actor in the world wanted to play Ted Hughes—one said to me that, to actors, Ted was like the 'Clint Eastwood of poets!' Daniel was one of the first actors we saw, and he kept returning to our minds. When Christine joined the film, she felt strongly that Daniel should play Ted—and when he read for her, he was so extraordinary that it became clear to us that nobody else could play the part."

Jeffs muses, "Daniel has a very intense energy. He's very raw and he has those piercing blue eyes. He can play complex and brooding—and you believe he is this poet, since he also had a bohemian feel about him. It was very exciting watching him and Gwyneth both fall into their characters and go on that journey and spark the way they did."

Craig followed his colleagues' lead on research—up to a point. He found that "there are so many people who've met Ted and they all have a different story to tell. I read a lot and talked to as many people as I could. In the end, as an actor, you have to make up your character because you can only take on so much."

Although the supporting roles in the project would be small ones, the filmmakers wanted high-caliber actors to play them. Blythe Danner, in real life the mother of Gwyneth Paltrow, was cast as Sylvia's mother, Aurelia Plath. Owen states, "We didn't cast Blythe just because she was Gwyneth's mother. They were both enthusiastic about it. She was perfect to play Aurelia." Jeffs adds, "It worked beautifully—the chemistry between them was clearly visible to everyone when we were working. It was fun and easy."

Danner reflects, "I've had the pleasure of playing Gwyneth's mother in three other projects before *Sylvia*, and they've all been very different and deeply gratifying. What amazes me is that I sometimes forget she's my daughter because Gwyneth has this extraordinary capability of becoming her character so completely. I enjoyed the subtlety of both the script and the performances; Daniel is also a marvelous actor."

Jared Harris signed on to play poet/editor Al Alvarez, friend and champion to both Sylvia and Ted. French actress Amira Casar was cast as Assia Wevill, the chance acquaintance who would later become a wrenching presence in the couple's lives together and apart.

Last but certainly not least, Sir Michael Gambon plays opposite Paltrow in delicate and even humorous one-on-one scenes as Sylvia's compassionate neighbor Professor Thomas. Owen states, "He's fantastic. Although they are painful, the scenes between Michael and Gwyneth were such a joy to watch—you rarely see two such wonderful performers interacting."

THE REALITY

For the *Sylvia* cast and crew, making a film about Sylvia Plath and Ted Hughes posed a new challenge at every stage of the process. The key question was, how closely to stick to the facts? The solution was, very closely—but with creative license applied to those private moments that can never truly be known or ascertained.

Alison Owen addressed these concerns early and often. She states, "You do have a duty to get things as right as possible, and I do feel a sense of responsibility for this personal history that grabbed me from the outset. With a real-life story, you cannot manipulate the narrative in the way that you can with a fictional story. On the other hand, I never said, 'We have to have a house that looks exactly like the one they lived in,' or became obsessive about details from Sylvia's diary. If you want to make a documentary-type film then that's fine, but that's not what we're doing here. Film to me has its own integrity; it's a work of art in its own right—the filmmakers are the artists and must take what they can from the subject and create their own version of what happened. They are not saying, 'This is the truth.' They are saying, 'This is what I'm getting from it and this is the story I want to tell.' It's always going to be a very personal account for the filmmakers. I don't think you should get obsessive about detail, but I do think you need to remain sensitive to it."

Christine Jeffs adds, "There is indeed that sense of responsibility, to be as truthful as you can to the people and their story. That was very important to us all. The details of Sylvia and Ted's story are what audiences will connect with. During filming, people who'd known them in real life came to visit the set and it was very moving to see these people be overwhelmed when they saw Gwyneth and Daniel. A lot of the shoot was very emotional."

John Brownlow, elaborating on the filmmaking team's approach, says, "This is a movie, not a documentary. Those people up on the screen are actors saying words that somebody else wrote, moving about on sets. We can't know what Ted and Sylvia really said to each other. That is not to say that we did not strive to be factually accurate, and more importantly, as emotionally truthful as we could possibly be. What a movie like *Sylvia* really aspires to is to get at some core truth, some nugget of understanding about its subject. That is what really matters, and I can put my hand on my heart and say that I think we've done so."

THE POETRY

At the creative heart of *Sylvia* is the emotional and aesthetic attachment of the filmmakers to the source material—the writings of Sylvia Plath and Ted Hughes.

John Brownlow based much of his screenplay on the feelings that the couple's poems inspired in him. He reports, "I made use of both of their poetry, Sylvia's in *Ariel* and Ted's in *Birthday Letters*, for emotional source material. That required me to find a biographical meaning in every line of every poem and as I did this I began to find the poems more and more profound. Sylvia's later poems, particularly from the moment she began to fully access her poetic gifts in Devon, are terrifyingly naked accounts of her own psychodrama, populated with the strange mythic creatures which I believe she used to make sense of the world. Once you start to understand who these fabulous creatures are and how they act, you can better understand Sylvia's actions late in life.

"Both of the works are subjective. *Birthday Letters* is also an emotional confessional, but what I found remarkable about it is that it uses the same language as Sylvia did to explain the same events. By the close of it, I really felt as though

I deeply understood these two people and could write about them with conviction."

As a teenager, Christine Jeffs discovered Sylvia Plath's work—and has been inspired ever since. She recalls, "I was into her as both a poet and a novelist; I had my own copies of *Ariel* and *The Bell Jar*, which have been well-thumbed over the years. She poured all her passion into her writing. I think people respond to that essence of her which she puts on the page; the detail and the energy of her writing are very strong."

Once in active preparation to play Sylvia, Gwyneth Paltrow gravitated towards the poems. She explains, "For a movie, I like to do a lot of reading about the subject. Sylvia Plath's poetry informed me more than the facts of her life. I found that, to play Sylvia, I could read a poem and it would put me exactly in the frame of mind and the emotional space that I needed to occupy. I know a lot about Sylvia, and I did a lot of research, but, artistically speaking, nothing was more helpful to me than her poetry."

Paltrow feels that Sylvia's work will always carry a strong message to the reader. She says, "In your early twenties, you have all these ideas about what you're supposed to be as a woman—what it means and what that's supposed to represent sociologically. You are at odds with whom you are inside—internally —and what the world expects you to be—externally. Sylvia was. The way she wrote resonates with young women because she was a person who was so in touch with her own identity, who she was, and what was happening within her. Inside, she felt that she was going mad; on the outside, she was showing a different persona.

"The lesson I take away from her work is that you have to integrate and be true to who you actually are; otherwise, you suffer. She was at once an artist, an intellectual, a sexual being, a mother, and a cook. She's very liberating to read because her writing accesses and connects you to the side of yourself that thinks you're capable of anything—of genius, or darkness. For a woman, that's very empowering."

Daniel Craig's interest in poetry—and not just Ted Hughes's—dates back to his childhood: "My dad reads a lot of poetry, and there's always been a lot of poetry in our house. I was bought a copy of Hughes's *Crow* when I was about twelve years old. It was a bit dense for me to read then, but it's definitely been part of my life. And I've long been aware of the mystique, rumor, and legend enveloping Sylvia and Ted.

"But I hadn't read any of Sylvia's work before starting *Sylvia*; that was always 'what girls read,' whilst the boys read Hughes—that was the divide. I found it a great experience to start reading Sylvia's stuff and join the circle."

Craig adds, "*Birthday Letters* is an enormous inspiration. Hughes kept his counsel for so long and never said anything or set the record straight about his life with Sylvia. You could say that he carries guilt, or you could say that his integrity is absolutely intact. I say the latter. You read *Birthday Letters* and you feel the love and passion that Ted felt for Sylvia. It was a difficult love and a great basis for our film—a passionate, tragic love affair makes for great viewing."

ABOUT SYLVIA PLATH

Sylvia Plath was born on October 27, 1932, in Jamaica Plain, Massachusetts.

Her father, Otto Plath, emigrated from Germany to the United States and became a biology professor at Boston University, specializing in the study of bees. Her mother, Aurelia Plath, taught German and English to high school students. Warren Plath was Sylvia's younger brother. The family lived in Winthrop, near Boston.

She had a comfortable childhood until her father died from complications due to undiagnosed diabetes, when she was eight years old—a loss that she would always feel. (Aurelia Plath died decades later, in 1987.)

Sylvia excelled in school. She was first published when a short couplet that she wrote—at the age of eight—was published in the *Boston (Sunday) Herald*. She sent her work to magazines for publication, and edited her school newspaper.

In her teenage years, she continually strived to get her poetry printed in major magazines and newspapers. Finally, after forty-five rejections, *Seventeen* published one of Sylvia's short stories, "And Summer Will Not Come Again." The magazine would publish her work again, and she was also soon published in *The Christian Science Monitor, Mademoiselle,* and *Harper's*, among other periodicals.

A member of the National Honor Society, Sylvia attended Smith College (in Northampton, Massachusetts) on scholarship. During the summer of her third year at Smith (1953), she was invited to be a guest editor for an issue of *Mademoiselle*. She would later dramatize her experiences in New York City during that time in her autobiographical novel *The Bell Jar.*

When she returned home, she learned that she had not been accepted to a fiction-writing course at Harvard. Shortly afterwards, on August 24, 1953, Sylvia tried to take her own life; after leaving a note saying that she had gone for a walk, she crawled under the house and swallowed an enormous dose of sleeping pills. After three days, she was discovered and rushed to McLean hospital. After treatments with intense psychotherapy and electroshock therapy, she returned to Smith for the second semester. She graduated summa cum laude in June 1955.

In October 1955, on a Fulbright Scholarship, Sylvia went abroad to Newnham College, Cambridge. She met Ted Hughes at a party on February 26, 1956. They married on June 16, 1956.

After she concluded her studies in the spring of 1957, Sylvia was offered a post at Smith College, which she accepted, returning to America with Ted. Prior to her starting work at Smith, Aurelia Plath gifted the couple with a holiday in Cape Cod, where they could spend the summer writing.

Excited at the prospect of teaching, Sylvia found the reality of it exhausting—with little time to pursue her writing. After one year of teaching, she did not return to the job. Instead, she worked as a receptionist in the psychiatric clinic of Massachusetts General Hospital in Boston. Secretly, she began to see therapist Ruth Boucher from McLean (where she had been hospitalized in 1953). She also attended an evening poetry class under the tutelage of Robert Lowell—who became an influence on her own poetry, which she was able to continue.

In December 1959, the couple returned to England and set up house in Primrose Hill. Sylvia was already pregnant, and gave birth to Frieda Rebecca Hughes on April 1, 1960. Her book of poetry *The Colossus* was published in October 1960. She had also begun writing *The Bell Jar,* and was pregnant again, but in February 1961 she miscarried.

The following summer, the Hughes family moved to Court Green in North Tawton, Devon. Sylvia and Ted's son, Nicholas Hughes, was born on January 17, 1962.

In July 1962, Sylvia discovered that Ted was having an affair with Assia Wevill, and the Hugheses separated that September. Over the following month, Sylvia wrote at least twenty-six of the *Ariel* poems.

In December, Sylvia took the children with her to London and moved to 23 Fitzroy Road, Primrose Hill, where the poet William Butler Yeats had once lived. The weather in the U.K. that winter was the coldest in over a century. On February 11, 1963, Sylvia committed suicide, dying by carbon monoxide poisoning from her gas oven. She was thirty years old.

The Bell Jar was first published in January 1963, not long before her death (and at that time under a pseudonym), but was not published in the United States until February 1971. *Time* magazine wrote, "Its most notable quality is an astonishing immediacy."

Ariel, the collection of poems that included much of her work from the fall of 1962, was published in 1965.

In 1982, two decades after her death, Sylvia Plath won the Pulitzer Prize for Poetry for the posthumously published *Collected Poems.*

ABOUT TED HUGHES

Edward (Ted) Hughes was born on August 17, 1930, in Mytholmroyd (in the U.K.'s Yorkshire Pennines).

He was the third child of William Hughes, a WWI veteran, and Edith Hughes. His father worked as a carpenter until they moved to Mexborough, a mining town, in 1937. There, after his mother came into a small inheritance, they opened a shop and sold newspapers, magazines, and tobacco. The storefront business allowed Ted to read comics and boys' magazines, which inspired his early storytelling.

Ted attended Mexborough Grammar School, where he studied Latin and began to write poetry. The 1944 Education Act had made it easier for Britons from any background to attend university, and in 1948 Ted won an Open Exhibition to Pembroke College, Cambridge. The start of Ted's studies there was delayed two years by his National Service in the RAF. In October 1951, he went up to Pembroke to study English, although he switched to archaeology and anthropology.

Following graduation, Ted went to live in London. He often returned to Cambridge, spending many a weekend with friends such as Michael Boddy and Lucas Myers. With the latter (and other peers), Ted conceived the literary magazine *St. Botolph's Review*, for which an inaugural party was arranged on February 26, 1956.

In a hall on the second floor of the Cambridge Women's Union, with a jazz band (featuring his friend Boddy on trombone) playing, Ted met Sylvia Plath for the first time. They were married less than four months later.

The couple moved to the United States the following year. Ted taught English and creative writing at the University of Massachusetts in Amherst from 1957 to 1959. By the time the Hugheses returned to England in late 1959, Ted had already been successfully published.

His work received a great deal of recognition from very early on in his career. His first collection, *The Hawk in the Rain,* won the Harper's Poetry Prize. His subsequent literary honors included the Whitbread Poetry award for *Tales From Ovid.*

Sylvia and Ted had two children together, but, by the time of their rural sojourn in Devon, they had become increasingly estranged. In September 1962, they separated after Sylvia had confirmed Ted's extramarital affair with Assia Wevill. In February 1963, Sylvia committed suicide.

With Assia, Ted fathered another child, named Shura, in 1965. Four years later, Assia killed herself and their daughter.

In 1970, Ted remarried, to Carol Orchard. In 1984, he became Poet Laureate, the highest honor that can be accorded a British poet.

For over three decades following her death, Ted Hughes refused to discuss Sylvia Plath and their years together. Then, in January 1998, he published *Birthday Letters*, a collection of poems about his life with Sylvia, for which he again won the Whitbread Poetry award. He died of cancer in October 1998, at the age of 68.

Among Ted's best-known works is his children's story "The Iron Giant," from 1968.

CAST AND CREW CREDITS

FOCUS FEATURES Presents

In Association with BBC FILMS CAPITOL FILMS and UK FILM COUNCIL

A RUBY FILMS PRODUCTION

GWYNETH PALTROW   DANIEL CRAIG

SYLVIA

Directed by
CHRISTINE JEFFS

Produced by
ALISON OWEN

Screenplay by
JOHN BROWNLOW

Executive Producers
DAVID M.THOMPSON
TRACEY SCOFFIELD
ROBERT JONES

Executive Producers
JANE BARCLAY
SHARON HAREL

Co-Producers
NERIS THOMAS

Director of Photography
JOHN TOON

Production Designer
MARIA DJURKOVIC

Editor
TARIQ ANWAR

Composer
GABRIEL YARED

Costume Designer
SANDY POWELL

Casting Director
KAREN LINDSAY STEWART

Line Producer
MARY RICHARDS

Associate Producer
PHIL RYMER

JARED HARRIS   AMIRA CASAR   ANDREW HAVILL   SAM TROUGHTON   LUCY DAVENPORT
ANTONY STRACHAN   with   BLYTHE DANNER   and   MICHAEL GAMBON

The Cast (in alphabetical order)

Morecambe . . . . David Birkin
Elizabeth . . . . Alison Bruce
Assia Wevill . . . . Amira Casar
Ted Hughes . . . . Daniel Craig
Aurelia Plath . . . . Blythe Danner
Doreen . . . . Lucy Davenport
James Michie . . . . Julian Firth
Mr. Robinson . . . . Jeremy Fowlds
Professor Thomas . . . . Michael Gambon
Ted's Cambridge Girlfriend . . . . . Sarah Guyler
Al Alvarez . . . . Jared Harris
David Wevill . . . . Andrew Havill
3rd Woman at Ted Hughes' Lecture . . . .
Theresa Healey
Martha Bergstrom . . . . Liddy Holloway
1st Woman at Ted Hughes' Lecture . . . .
Robyn Malcolm
Charles Langridge . . . . Michael Mears
Young American Girl Student . . . . Siobhan Page
Sylvia Plath . . . . Gwyneth Paltrow
Vicar . . . . Derek Payne
Midwife . . . . Sonia Ritter

Telegram Boy . . . . Billie Seymour
Michael Boddy . . . . Antony Strachan
Myra Norris . . . . Katherine Tozer
Tom Hadley-Clarke . . . . Sam Troughton
Infant Frieda . . . . Eliza Wade
Baby Nicholas . . . . Ben & Joel Want
Tom's Girlfriend . . . . Hannah Watkins
2nd Woman at Ted Hughes' Lecture . . . .
Tandi Wright

The Crew

Directed by . . . . Christine Jeffs
Produced by . . . . Alison Owen
Screenplay by . . . . John Brownlow
Executive Producers . . . . . David M. Thompson
Tracey Scoffield
Robert Jones
Executive Producers . . . . Jane Barclay
Sharon Harel
Co-Producer . . . . Neris Thomas

Director of Photography . . . . John Toon
Production Designer . . . . . . Maria Djurkovic

Editor . . . . Tariq Anwar
Composer . . . . Gabriel Yared
Costume Designer . . . . Sandy Powell
Casting Director . . . . . . Karen Lindsay Stewart
Line Producer . . . . Mary Richards
Associate Producer . . . . Phil Rymer
1st Assistant Director . . . . Richard Styles
Sound Recordist . . . . David Crozier
Supervising Art Director . . . . John Hill
Set Decorator . . . . Philippa Hart
Chief Hairdresser . . . . Kay Georgiou
Chief Makeup Artist . . . . Rebecca Lafford
Financial Controller . . . . Shruti Shah
Location Managers . . . . Ben Rimmer
Adam Richards
Post-Production Supervisor . . . . . . Meg Clark
Supervising Sound Editor . . Christopher Ackland
Focus Puller . . . . Mark Milsome
Clapper Loader . . . . Harry Bowers
Grip . . . . Mark Binnall
Video Assist . . . . Benjamin Croce
FT2 Trainee . . . . Jani Jance
Script Supervisor . . . . Cathy Doubleday
Sound Maintenance . . . . John Casali
Sound Assistant . . . . James Harris
Choreographer . . . . Jack Murphy
Dialogue Coach . . . . Julia Wilson-Dixon
Unit Manager . . . . Claire Tovey
Location Assistant . . . . Paul Rimmer
Location Scouts . . . Phil Clark, Becky Chambers
Cornwall Location . . . . Johnny Bamford
Production Coordinator . . . . . . Patsy De Lord
Ruby Films Coordinator . . . . Iona Price
Assistant to Alison Owen . . . . Faye Ward
Assistant to Christine Jeffs . . . . . Tonia Wright
Assistant to Gwyneth Paltrow . . . . Jenny Turner
Production Assistant . . . . . . Rachel Wardlow
Production Runner . . . . . . Emily Ann Sonnet
Researcher . . . . Tanya Shaw
Script Editor . . . . Joan E. Scheckel
Script Clearance . . . . Tim Carter
Development Executive for Ruby Films . . . . . .
Nicki Sung
Accountant for Ruby Films . . . . . Suku Samanta

Post-Production Accountant . . . . Peta Inglesent
1st Assistant Accountant . . . . . . Matt Dalton
2nd Assistant Accountant . . . . . Isaac Sananes
2nd Assistant Director . . . . Carlos Fidel
3rd Assistant Director . . . . . Caroline Chapman
Crowd Casting . . . . Candy Marlowe
Floor Runners . . . . . Samar Pollitt, Lester Lloyd
Casting of Children . . . . Buffy Kirkpatrick
Child Coach . . . . Suzanne Anderson

Unit Publicity . . . . McDonald & Rutter
Unit Publicist . . . . Claudia Kalindjian
Stills Photographers . . . David Appleby, Bill Kaye
Art Director . . . . Jane Cecchi
Production Buyer . . . . Nicola Barnes
Standby Art Director . . . . Joanna Foley
Assistant Art Director . . . . Emily Lutyens
Draughtsman . . . . Dean Clegg
Makeup & Hair Artist . . . . Tracey Lee
Wardrobe Supervisor . . . . Clare Spragge
Assistant Costume Designer . . . . Kay Manasseh
Wardrobe Assistants . . . . Andrew Hunt
Sunita Singh
Additional Wardrobe Assistants . . . .
Joseph Kowalewski, Sophie Norinder
1st Assistant Editor . . . . Saska Simpson
Dialogue/ADR Editors . . . . Nigel Mills,
Steve Mayer, Tariq Anwar
Sound Conform Editor . . . . Nigel Stone
Foley Editor . . . . Jacques Leroide
Additional Post-Production Supervision . . . . . .
Russ Woolnough, Tony Tromp

For BBC Films
Production Executive . . . . Michael Wood
Production Finance Coordinator . . . Nick Savva
Script Executive . . . . Jamie Laurenson

For U.K. Film Council
Head of Physical Production . . . Fiona Morham
Production Executive . . . . Luke Morris
Production Executive . . . . Brock Norman Brock

Property Master . . . . Ty Teiger
Props Storeman . . . . Brian West
Chargehand Propman . . . . . . Martin Kingsley
Chargehand Standby Propman . . Bernard Hearne
Standby Propman . . . . Matthew Foster
Dressing Propman . . . . Peter Watson
Junior Propman . . . . Alex King
Gaffer Electrician . . . . . Robert "Chuck" Finch
Rigging Gaffer Electrician . . . . . Billy Merrell
Best Boy . . . . Steve Finch
Electricians . . . . Richard Merrell,
Perry Cullen, Wick Finch
Generator Operator . . . . Dave Bruce
Construction Manager . . . . John Bohan
Asst Construction Manager . . . . Thomas Martin
Supervising Carpenter . . . . . Daniel O'Regan
Chargehand Carpenter . . . . . . John O'Brien
Carpenters . . . . . Peter Brown, Gavin Gordon,
David Lowery, Anthony McGee,
Eamon McLoughlin, Peter Nodwell,
Geoff Nolan, Matt Whelan, David Youngs

142

Wood Machinist . . . . Steve Weston	Clapper Loader . . . . Sean Kelly
Trainee Carpenter . . . . Roy O'Brien	Video Operator . . . . Carissa Jamieson
Hod Painter . . . . Clive Ward	Key Grip . . . . Brian Harris
Chargehand Painter . . . . Alan Grenham	Grips . . . . Oli Harris, Ben Bell
Painters . . . . John Cloke, Michael Finlay,	Boom Operator . . . . Hugo Tichborne
Graham Pierce, Doug Regan,	2nd Unit Camera . . . . Nick Hutchinson
Geoff Sullivan, Ken Welland	2nd Unit Camera Assistant . . . . . . Angus Ward
Supervising Stagehand . . . . . . Michael Webb	Production Account . . . . Liz Goddard
Stagehands . . . . . David Jones, Terry Meadows,	Production Coordinator . . . . Laura Fong
Eddie O'Neill	Production Assistants. . Bex Coomer, Lucy Jordan
Chargehand Rigger. . . . . Alan Williams	Production Runner . . . . Nathan Sim
Riggers . . . . . . Fred Crawford, Chris Hawkins,	Set Production Runner . . . . Kate Stalker
Martin Hawkins	Unit Manager. . . . . Gordon Fawcett
Construction Electricians . . . . . . James McGee	Unit Assistant. . . . . Debra Duncan
Joe McGee	Location Scouts . . . David Curtis, Dale Gardiner
Construction Driver . . . . . . Richard Magennis	Set Dresser. . . . . Chris Elliot
Standby Carpenter . . . . Joe Alley	Props Buyer Standby . . . . Mark Grenfell
Standby Painter . . . . Perry Bell	Props Standby Assistant . . . Anthony Catermoule
Standby Rigger. . . . . Martin Goddard	Assistant Props Buyer . . . . . . Elizabeth Goodall
Stunt Coordinator . . . . Jim Dowdall	Art Dept.' Coordinator . . . . Kim Turner
Stunt Performers. . . . . Bean Peel, Steve Street	Art Dept.' Runner . . . . Sarah Goodall
Unit Drivers . . . . Alan Bradshaw,	Scenic Artist. . . . . Trevor Lithgow
Jimmy Carruthers, Jeremy Jacobs	Scenic Artist Assistant. . . . . . . Leon Lithgow
Ms. Paltrow's Driver . . . . Colin Morris	Construction Manager . . . . Ken Turner
Mr. Craig's Driver . . . . Steve Mitchard	Carpenters . . . . . Mike Appleby, Bradley Diack,
Camera Car Driver. . . . . Russell King	Rex Turner
Wardrobe Driver . . . . Roy Hopkins	Laborer. . . . . Karl Holland
Standby Prop Driver . . . . Mick Boddy	Greensman . . . . Ron Turner
Standby Construction Driver . . . Eddie Saunders	Greensman Assistant. . . . . Niven Hislop
Facility Drivers . . . . Laurence Duncan,	Vehicle Wrangler . . . . Justin Cardon
Richard Ong, Duncan Prentice	Food Stylist . . . . Simon Niak
Minibus Drivers . . . . Ian Drinkwater	Wardrobe Supervisor . . . . . . Kirsty Cameron
Gavin Mullins	Wardrobe Assistants . . . . Pip O'Brien,
Stand-In for Ms. Paltrow . . . . Collette Appleby	Jenny Ruston, Melody Newton,
Stand-In for Mr. Craig. . . . . . . Nick Hussey	Emily Barr, Violet Faigon
Catering. . . . . Premier Caterers Limited	Makeup & Hair. . . . Dominie Till, Abby Collins
Catering Manager . . . . Carole Bulmer	Additional Makeup & Hair . . . . . Denise Kum,
Chefs . . . . . . Fred Cooper, Robert Gregory	Jane O'Kane, Barbie Cope,
Catering Assistants. . . . . . . Christine Perrett,	Anita Brolley, Louise Dignan-Smith,
Anita Hughes, Kim Marsh, Les Perrett,	Kimberley McLean, Michelle Barber
Justin Goodman	Casting Assistant . . . . Cindy Diver
Health & Safety Officer . . . . . Cyril Gibbons	2nd Assistant Director . . . . Hamish McFarlane
Unit Nurse . . . . Paula Oehlers	3rd Assistant Director . . . . Sam Long
	Special Effects Supervisor . . . . . . Ken Durey
New Zealand Shoot	Special Effects Technician . . . . . Barry McGinn
Line Producer. . . . . Ian Gibbons	Gaffer. . . . . Brett Mills
1st Assistant Director . . . . Chris Short	Best Boy . . . . Max Catterick
Production Manager. . . . . Su Hucks	Electrician . . . . Sol Bollinger
Supervising Art Director. . . . . . . Iain Aitken	Lighting Assistant. . . . . Daniel Wilson
Production Sound Mixer . . . . . David Madigan	Generator Operator . . . . Joe Bollinger
Location Manager . . . . . . Harry Whitehurst	Unit Generator Operator . . . . . . Chris Ruane
Casting . . . . Maya Dalziel	Stunt Doubles . . . . Dana Porter, Alan Poppleton
Steadicam Operator . . . . . Cameron McLean	Stand-Ins . . . . . Kristine Gullick, James Hunter,
Focus Puller . . . . Dean McCarroll	Caroline Cook

Safety Officer . . . . Rolf Crausaz
Water Safety . . . . Gary Butt
Nurse . . . . Polly Dickson
Catering . . . . Flying Trestles
Special Chef . . . . Chiyumi Naito
Security . . . . Paul Ropata, Peter Taggart
Transportation Manager . . . . . . Don Anderson
Drivers . . . . . Doug Crighton, Eddie Clements,
        Mike Ford, Brian Illingworth,
        Anthony Moore, Alan Pegley,
        Maurice Ranginiwa, Alan Richardson,
        Steven Roe, Andy South

Auckland Shoot Additional Crew
Location Manager . . . . Clayton Tikoo
Production Runner . . . . . Donna McConnell
Unit Manager . . . . Marco Majorama
Focus Puller . . . . Bryony Matthews
Clapper Loader . . . . Aletia Hudson
Water Safety . . . . Willy Heatley
Drivers . . . . Mark Prowse, Chris Couch
Security . . . . Jason Brott

With Many Thanks to:
        The Kati Huirapa Runaka Ki Puketeraki
        Dunedin City Council
        Peter Harris
        Pakiri Beach - Laly Haddon

Digital Visual Effects by The Moving Picture Company
Head of Production . . . . Michael Elson
Visual Effects Producer . . . . Stefan Drury
Visual Effects Supervisors . . . . . Jessica Norman
                Tom Wood
Visual Effects Coordinator . . . . . Sally Spencer
Compositors . . . . Mark Curtis, Doug Larmour,
        Stuart Lashley, Niki Wakefield

Titles Designed by . . . . Matt Curtis, AP
Digital Titles & Opticals by . . . . . Cineimage
Optical and Title Supervision . . . . . Steve Boag
                Martin Bullard
Digital Compositing . . . . . Matthew Symonds
Optical Camera . . . . Dave Gurney
Off-Line Auto Conform . . . . Fabienne Arbogast
Client Liaison . . . . Kerrie Gant
Sound Re-Recorded at . . . . Goldcrest
                Post-Production Facilities
Re-Recording Mixers . . . . Paul Carr
                Andrew Thompson
ADR Recordist . . . . Robert Farr
Voice Casting . . . . . Brendan Donnison MPSE
                Vanessa Baker

Foley Artists . . . . . Peter Burgess, Andy Derrick

Music
Composed and Conducted by . . . Gabriel Yared
Orchestrated by . . . . . Gabriel Yared, John Bell
Additional Orchestrations by . . . . Nick Ingham
Music Supervising . . . .
        Jean-Pierre Arquié / Film Music Service
Synthesiser Programming & Realization . . . . .
        Nathaniel Méchaly / NX Studio, Paris
Recorded & Mixed by . . . . Peter Cobbin
                at Abbey Road Studios, London
Assistants . . . . . Andrew Dudman, Mirek Stiles
Orchestra Contractor . . . . Isobel Griffiths
Orchestra Leader . . . . Rolf Wilson
Cello . . . . Anthony Pleeth
Oboe . . . . David Thodore
Cor Anglais . . . . Sue Bohling
Clarinet . . . . Nicolas Bucknall
Keyboards . . . . Gabriel Yared
Music Editor . . . . Sophie Cornet

Special Thanks to:
        Colette Barber and all the Staff
        at Abbey Road Studios,
        Chantal Bouiges, Xavier Dreyfuss, Nick Mera &
        Dave Hague (Dakota), Pierre Khanna-Smith,
        Samantha Richards, Leila Stacey

Laboratory Contact . . . . John Ensby
Grader . . . . Peter Hunt
Negative Cutter . . . . . Reelskill Film Cutting
        Limited / Eddy Kolkiewicz, Andy Robinson
Dolby Consultant . . . . Richard Welsh
Camera and Lenses Supplied by . . . . Arri-Media
Lighting Equipment Supplied by . . . Lee Lighting
Editing Equipment Supplied by . . . .
                London Editing Machines
Telecine Facilities (U.K.) . . . .
                Midnight Transfer / John Kerr
Telecine Facilities (New Zealand) . . . . Oktobor
Laboratory (U.K.) . . . . Technicolor
Laboratory (New Zealand) . . Atlab New Zealand
Film Stock . . . . Kodak Limited
Stills Processing . . . . Blow-Up
Post Production Services . . . . Postmatters
Completion Guaranty Provided by . . . .
        International Film Guarantors / Luke Randolph

Insurance Services . . . . Aon / Albert G. Ruben,
                Kevin O'Shea
Legal Services . . . . Billy Hinshelwood
Freight Services (U.K.) Supplied by . . . .
                Dynamic Int Freight Services

Freight Services (New Zealand)Xtreme Forwarding
Transport Services. . . Lays International Limited,
Studio Workshops Limited
Facility Vehicles . . . . Location Facilities Limited
Costumes Supplied by . . Angels The Costumiers
Wig Makers/Suppliers . . . Owen, King & Turner
Snow Effects Supplied by. . . . . Snow Business

Made On Location in The U.K.
In London, Cambridge, Cornwall and
At Shepperton Studios, London, England
And in
Dunedin, New Zealand

With Special Thanks to:
Elizabeth Sigmund, Al Alvarez, Jane Wright, Isabel
Begg, Hannah Leader, Will Evans, Vince Holden,
James Schamus, Glenn Williamson, Avy Eschenasy,
Kevin Hyman, Jeff Roth, Peter Touche, Robin
Hilton, Ingenious Films Limited, Nigel Palmer,
Jackie Hurt, Richard Arnold, John Baldwin,
Michael Elson and The Moving Picture Company,
Jackie Rowden, Philip Cooper, Gary Stone

"Henry King" by Hilaire Belloc
Quoted by Permission of PFD on Behalf of The
Estate of Hilaire Belloc

"The Sorrow Of Love" by W.B. Yeats
Quoted by Permission of The Society of Authors
on Behalf of
The Estate of W.B.Yeats

"Gunga Din" by Rudyard Kipling
Quoted by Kind Permission of AP Watt on Behalf
of
The Estate of Rudyard Kipling

"The Quaker Graveyard In Nantucket"
Recorded by Robert Lowell
Copyright © 1976 by Robert Lowell
Used with the Permission of The Wylie Agency,
Inc.
Recording Taken from The Yale Series of
Recorded Poets
by Permission of The Department of English
and The Yale Collection of Historical Sound
Recordings,
Yale University Music Library

"Hey Doc"
Performed by The Inkspots
Written by Kim Gannon and Edgar Sampson

© WB Music Corp
by Kind Permission of Warner/Chappell Music
Limited
Courtesy of Jasmine Records

Made with the Support of the
U.K. Film Council Premiere Fund

While this motion picture is based on a true story certain character names have been changed, some main characters have been composited or invented and a number of incidents fictionalized.

Dolby SR/SRD, in selected theaters

Aspect Ratio: 2:35/1 [Scope]

MPAA Rating: R (for sexuality/nudity and language)

www.sylviamovie.com

A Focus Features Release

About the Filmmakers

Christine Jeffs (Director) was born in Lower Hutt, New Zealand. She graduated from Massey University with a B.A. in sociology and geography.

Jeffs entered the film industry to work in post-production sound. Becoming an assistant editor, she worked on several New Zealand documentaries as well as such feature films as Melanie Read's *Send a Gorilla*, Gaylene Preston's *Ruby and Rata*, John Laing's *Absent Without Leave*, and Alison Maclean's *Crush* (starring Marcia Gay Harden). In 1990, she completed a diploma in editing at the Australian Film, Television and Radio School and began cutting films as well as commercials.

Her first short film, *Stroke*, which she wrote, directed, and edited, was screened at numerous film festivals including Cannes and Sundance. Her first feature film, *Rain*, for which she adapted the screenplay from Kirsty Gunn's novel, was selected for its World Premiere in the Directors Fortnight at the 2001 Cannes International Film Festival. After enjoying great acclaim at Cannes, *Rain* was invited to screen all over the world at other film festivals, including Edinburgh, Melbourne, Toronto, and Sundance. Concurrent with its screening at the latter film festival in January 2002, Ms. Jeffs was named one of *Daily Variety*'s "10 Directors to Watch."

Jeffs has also had a very successful career as a commercials director. In 1999, she topped the New Zealand *ADMEDIA* poll of creative directors' vote for Best New Zealand Director. For her commercials work, she has been honored with numerous awards, including multiple AXIS Awards and a Bronze Lion at Cannes.

She next plans to direct *Wildlife*, from her screenplay adaptation of Richard Ford's novel.

Alison Owen (Producer), producer (partnered with Working Title Films) of Shekhar Kapur's *Elizabeth*, was nominated for an Academy Award when the film became a Best Picture finalist. The film was nominated for six additional Oscars, winning in the Best Makeup category. *Elizabeth* was also nominated for twelve BAFTA Awards, and won five. As producer, Owen was honored with the BAFTA win of the Alexander Korda Award for Best British Film.

Owen was educated at University College, London, and worked in various capacities in production, distribution, and development before becoming a producer. She first produced pop music promos/videos and commercials. She next worked on documentaries and in television before beginning film projects. Her television successes included the U.K. series *Diary of a Teenage Health Freak*, which won the RTS Award for Best Youth Programme, and *End of an Era* which won the Silver Rose at the Montreux Festival and was nominated for a BAFTA Award.

She produced her first feature, *Hear My Song*, in 1991. Directed by Peter Chelsom, and starring Ned Beatty, Adrian Dunbar, and Tara Fitzgerald, it was nominated for Golden Globe and BAFTA Awards and won Best Comedy Film at the British Comedy Awards. Owen was nominated as Most Promising New Producer by the Producers Guild of America.

Ms. Owen then set up shop at Working Title, where she established a low-budget film division. She returned to producing with *The Young Americans*, starring Harvey Keitel and directed by Danny Cannon. She next produced David Anspaugh's *Moonlight and Valentino*, which marked her first collaboration with *Sylvia* star Gwyneth Paltrow; *Roseanna's Grave*, directed by Paul Weiland and starring Jean Reno and Mercedes Ruehl; and the globally successful *Elizabeth*, which was the breakthrough film for its star, Cate Blanchett.

Partnering with *Sylvia* co-producer Neris Thomas, she inaugurated the production company Ruby Films in January 1999. Ruby has thus far made Steve Barron's *Rat* (starring Pete Postlethwaite); Menhaj Huda's *Is Harry on the Boat?* (starring Danny Dyer); Philippa Collie-Cousins' *Happy Now?* (for BBC Films, starring Paddy Considine); and *Sylvia*.

Owen is currently at work on *Proof*, the film version of David Auburn's Pulitzer Prize-winning play, starring Gwyneth Paltrow for director John Madden; Dominic Savage's *Love & Hate*; and *Tulip Fever*, to be directed by John Madden from Tom Stoppard's screenplay adaptation of Deborah Moggach's novel, with Jude Law and Keira Knightley starring. Her future Ruby projects as producer also include Sandra Goldbacher's *Faith*; *Siege of Krishnanpur*, with Working Title Films; and *Rachel's Holiday*, with BBC Films.

Separately from Ruby, she is executive-producing Edgar Wright's *Shaun of the Dead*, which is in post-production.

John Brownlow (Screenwriter) was born in Lincoln, England, and went to Oxford to study mathematics. However, after a year, he decided that he no longer wished to know what x equalled, and switched to English literature—against the advice of his elders and betters.

After graduation, he worked briefly as a photographer before beginning a career in television documentaries as an investigative journalist.

During the 1990s, Brownlow rose to become one of Britain's best-known documentary filmmakers, producing and directing several highly acclaimed documentary series for Channel 4, including *Pennies From Bevan*, *School Rules*, *Canterbury Tales*, *Deadly Experiments*, and *Navy Blues*.

In 1999, on the strength of scripts written "on spec," he switched to working as a full-time screenwriter for film companies in London and Los Angeles. *Sylvia*, which he began work on in late 2000, is his first screenplay to have been filmed.

Brownlow has several screenplays slated for production in 2003 and 2004, including *Alias Grace* (based on the Margaret Atwood novel, with Working Title Films), *The Numbers Man* (with Bel Air Entertainment), *London Fear* (to be directed by Kari Skogland), *Marlowe* (with Natural Nylon), and *The Phoenix* (about the Hindenburg, with Kennedy/Marshall Films).

In association with *Sylvia* producer Alison Owen he is also developing his feature film directorial debut, *The Death of Sweet Mister*, which he is adapting from Daniel Woodrell's novel.

In 2003, he was named one of *Daily Variety*'s "10 Screenwriters to Watch."